Implementing and Improving Teaming:
A Handbook for Middle Level Leaders

IMPLEMENTING AND IMPROVING TEAMING

A Handbook for Middle Level Leaders

by
Jerry Rottier

National Middle School Association
Columbus, Ohio

National Middle School Association
2600 Corporate Exchange Drive, Suite 370
Columbus, Ohio 43231
Telephone (800) 528-NMSA

Printed in the United States of America

NMSA Stock Number: 1234

Second Printing July 1997

L B
1029
.T4
R68
1996
cpm.1998

Library of Congress Cataloging-in-Publication Data

Rottier, Jerry.

   Implementing and improving teaming: a handbook for middle level leaders/Jerry Rottier
   Includes bibliographical references (p.)
   ISBN 1-56090-110-1

1. Teaching teams--United States--Handbooks, manuals, etc.

2. Middle schools--United States--Handbooks, manuals, etc.

I. Title

LB1029.T4R68   1996

371.1'48--dc20   98-8797

Contents

About the Author

Jerry Rottier, a charter member of National Middle School Association, has been active in middle level education throughout the United States presenting at conferences, providing workshops, and consulting with school districts. He teaches graduate and undergraduate courses in middle level education at the University of Wisconsin-Eau Claire. Dr. Rottier has written articles on middle level issues and co-authored a book on cooperative learning. He also directs The Center for Middle Level Assessment which provides assessment services to middle schools.

———

Special appreciation is extended to Kim Rottier for the original artwork and to Amy Hartfeldt for her assistance with editing and formatting.

Introduction

T eaming has become the dominant organizational pattern in middle schools. The complexity of educational demands made on schools and the curriculum no longer supports the one teacher-one group of students-one subject model. Teams of teachers, sharing their knowledge, skills, and philosophies are the organizational model to lead our schools into the next century. Some middle schools need assistance in the initial implementation of teaming; others are ready for refining the process to realize the full benefits of teaming. We need to move beyond celebrating the organization of teams and exploit all the potential that teams have for improving the achievement of students.

Chapter 1 provides the backdrop for the remainder of the book by sharing the rationale for teaming. The many benefits that accrue to both students and teachers, and to the curriculum and instruction practices are presented.

Reviewing the various arrangements of teams in a middle school is one component of Chapter 2. The other component challenges middle schools to consider new organizational arrangements that will include all teachers on teams, improve communication, and develop more opportunities for connections across the curriculum.

Scheduling is the theme of Chapter 3. Special attention is given to block scheduling which fosters creative approaches to making time support instructional goals.

Often forgotten in the development of the middle school has been the team leader. Clarifying and strengthening this role on a team may be the single greatest factor in the movement toward high performance teams. Responsibilities of this emerging role are explained in Chapter 4.

The principal plays a key role in developing and nurturing teams. The principal's understanding and commitment to teaming will have a direct bearing on its effectiveness. With the leadership of the principal, working in concert with team leaders, teams will have a greater opportunity to achieve their potential. These topics are shared in Chapter 5.

Chapter 6 explores some of the fundamental characteristics of effective teams. It challenges teams to establish measurable goals and to determine the extent to which they have been achieved. How to make team meetings more effective is clarified. The various stages of development that teams go through on their journey to high performance are explained.

Staff development is mandatory if teaming is to produce intended results. Stages of staff development, from the initial understanding to setting expectations for students, are shared in Chapter 7. Suggestions are provided for scheduling team meetings.

Chapter 8 focuses on a difficult topic, dysfunctional teams. Bringing a small group of professionals together to function as a team does not always result in harmonious relationships. Three levels of managing dysfunctional teams are explored along with suggestions on conflict resolution procedures.

Two major skills of teaming, decision making and problem solving, are the central elements of Chapter 9. In addition, analytic tools to assist problem solving are presented. Teams that master these skills will make a difference in their performance.

Moving to a higher level of effectiveness with teaming requires attention to goals, the refinement of decision-making and problem-solving skills, the ability to handle dysfunctional teams, and clarifying the roles of team leaders and principals. It requires a dedication to make teaming a vehicle for improving the curriculum and instruction for students. These changes may cause some discomfort for established teams.

The middle school community has learned a great deal with the implementation of teaming over the past two decades. We have learned that teaming can have a very positive effect on students' attitudes and on achievement. We have learned that teachers in teams reach a higher level of professionalism and experience greater personal satisfaction. We have learned that the opportunities for connecting and integrating the curriculum are enhanced significantly with teams. We have learned these things largely through trial and error by dedicated personnel in middle schools. However, we must not stop learning and accept the status of teaming as it stands presently. We need to improve all facets of teaming if we are to meet the demands of teaching and learning in middle level schools in the twenty-first century. ❏

1

Teaming in the Middle School

*Companies in the 1990s are realizing that a di-
verse group of people – using their own creativity, innovation, judgment, intuition and brain
power – can do a better job in today's world of
constant change than any set of formal procedures,
methods, or controls administered by a remote,
centralized management.*

– Thomas A. Kayser

Today's society, with change as the only constant, demands organiza-
tions that can embrace and respond to change. If middle schools
are to meet the demands of the 1990s and provide leadership for the
next century, organizational arrangements of schools must change just as they
are changing in the business world. In middle schools, these changes will bring
individuals together to work as teams and establish a climate of colleagiality.

Peter Scholtes (1992), says: "... rarely does a single person have enough knowledge or experience to understand everything that goes on in a process. Therefore, major gains in quality and productivity most often result from teams – a
group of people pooling their skills, talents, and knowledge." This statement,
describing the synergism teams create, must become the *modus operandi* to
improve teaching and learning in a middle school.

Teaching is itself an increasingly complex task. In an age when information
is doubling every two years, teaching students how to retrieve, analyze, synthe-
size, and evaluate information must become a focal point of the curriculum.
When technology is expanding at an astronomical rate, being able to incorpo-
rate technology into the instructional program is a significant challenge. When
society has a growing number of one-parent families and families with both
parents working outside the home, dealing with young adolescents and their
unique needs is especially challenging.

Teachers are already overextended and cannot be expected to work longer and harder, but they can be placed on teams where they can work smarter. Putting teachers with complementary knowledge and skills on a team results in amassing talent that exceeds the capabilities of any single teacher. Teams of teachers can be more responsive to changing events and demands than an individual or an entire institution.

An interdisciplinary organization provides many advantages for students, teachers, communication, and for curriculum and instruction within the school.

Advantages for Students

Teaming brings together several teachers and a common group of students, creating a small caring family as suggested in *Turning Points – Preparing American Youth for the 21st Century* (1989). Teachers come to know their students very well, and students become comfortable with a small group of teachers. Interacting with a small group of students ensures that fewer students will go unnoticed. Teachers are more cognizant of changes in student behavior and can offer assistance when needed. Every child in this family environment will come to know at least one adult well. In time of need or personal trauma, it is important that students feel confident approaching an adult for assistance. These two possibilities – teachers knowing students and students knowing teachers – offer excellent opportunities for developing a climate in which academic learning and personal growth can occur.

Advantages for Teachers

When a team of two to five teachers is aligned with approximately 50-125 students, a consistent set of classroom management procedures can be established. Uniformity in the ways used to deal with such matters as being tardy, leaving the classroom, chewing gum, and covering books will benefit early adolescents who are already confused on a number of issues. When several teachers decide collectively how to handle the problems of particular students and then work together to implement their plan, the potential is great for changing the behavior of these students. In like manner, consistency in routine instructional procedures such as late work, makeup work, and coordination of due dates will be valuable for both students and teachers. Ways of assessing

and reporting student progress will be most effective when developed coopera-
tively by the team and communicated to students and parents.

A great sense of professionalism among teachers develops through teaming.
Heretofore, teachers seldom met with one another to discuss professional issues. Now during common planning time, team members assist and support
one another. Working together to
help a student overcome a difficult problem improves all
teachers' competence.
Providing assistance to
others when needed
generates confidence
and self-esteem. Uti-
lizing the strengths
of one another cre-
ates synergy on the
team.

Teaming provides opportunities for teacher involvement in decision making
and leadership. It challenges teachers to take a leadership role in making decisions about curriculum and instruction to benefit students. Teams involved in
the hiring process and structuring the induction program for beginning teachers
are engaged in a professional activity. Involvement in these two areas strengthens the relationship between teachers and administration.

When teachers work as a team, they come to understand students' behavior
better, assist one another in growing professionally, and experience a much
higher level of satisfaction and enjoyment with their work.

Advantages for Communication

In a teaming structure, common planning time provides opportunities for teachers to communicate with and tap the expertise of counselors, special education
teachers, media specialists, and the administration. Perhaps the greatest opportunity for improved communication is between team and special education personnel. Constant interaction between regular and special education teachers
benefits all students on the team, not only the special education students.

Communication with parents is significantly more effective when a team is involved. Discussing a student situation before contacting the parents is valuable. When they can meet with several teachers at one time, benefits accrue to both parents and teachers. Progress reports are appreciated; by making this type of communication a team effort, the chance of parents' receiving regular proficiency reports is enhanced.

Advantages for the Curriculum

Many, if not most, students view the curriculum as a set of disjointed and disconnected experiences. In a middle school with an interdisciplinary organization, teachers not only become aware of the content of various disciplines as a result of meeting with colleagues on a regular basis but they make connections. Teaming allows the coordination of teaching learning skills such as reading, problem solving, and information retrieval. Knowing the topics to be taught in other disciplines, teachers can sequence

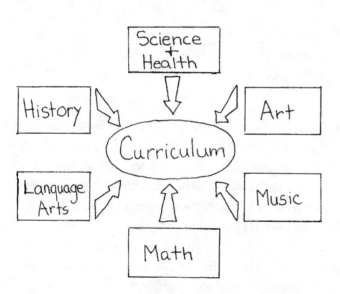

their curriculum to teach related topics at the same time. This leads to discovering opportunities to integrate the curriculum. Having a group of teachers regularly discuss the curriculum can result in significant changes in the content and instruction provided students and is potentially the greatest benefit to be derived from teaming.

SUMMARY

Teaming allows people to work in new ways to stay abreast of the informational and technological society in which we live. It brings new demands for teachers and administrators. Learning how to work together rather than alone and to make decisions and solve problems collectively are new challenges. Teaming requires a commitment to change which will not come easily for some. Yet the possibilities created with a teaming arrangement are so numerous and desirable, *all* middle level schools need to give serious thought to its full implementation. For those middle schools with teaming in place, the time is appropriate to raise the quality of teaming to a much higher level of effectiveness and efficiency. ❑

2

Team Designs

The student should, upon entering middle grade school, join a small community in which people – students and adults – get to know each other well to create a climate for intellectual development.
— *Turning Points: Preparing American Youth for the 21st Century*

M any factors affect the design of teams in a middle school. Because each middle school is different, it is important to understand these designs in order to create the most effective teams. This chapter focuses on team arrangements involving mathematics, science, social studies, and language arts plus several arrangements that include one or more encore courses. In addition, a number of designs that place all teachers on teams are described.

The term "core" used here, refers to mathematics, science, social studies, and language arts courses. All remaining courses in the middle school are termed "encore." This is an attempt to move away from designations such as academic/nonacademic, academic/related arts, and core/exploratory all of which imply, unfairly, a hierarchy.

CORE/ENCORE TEAM DESIGNS

Two-Teacher Team

The two-teacher team, Figure 1, is used quite often in grade six as a sound transition from a single-teacher, self-contained classroom in the elementary school to the four- or five-teacher team usually found in grades seven and eight. In this arrangement, one teacher has primary responsibility for math and science, while the second teacher has responsibility for social studies and lan-

guage arts, and each may teach a section of reading. Courses taught by each
teacher can depend on the strengths and interests of each one. Both teachers
would need multiple certification or a general elementary certification allowing them to teach all subjects. This model allows one teacher and a group of
students to spend a larger portion of the day together, strengthening the bond
between them. Time can be used more flexibly, and more opportunities are
available to integrate the curriculum.

Figure 1

Two-Teacher Team

50-60 Students	
TEACHER A	TEACHER B
Math	Social Studies
Math	Social Studies
Science	Language Arts
Science	Language Arts
Reading	Reading

Three-Teacher Team

The three-teacher team, Figure 2, is similar to the two-teacher team, except
that all teachers teach one subject by themselves and a section of the two remaining subjects. Others ways of dividing the instructional responsibilities are
also possible. It requires three teachers with multiple certification or general
certification. As with the two-teacher team, students stay with one team member for a period of time. This model provides for more flexible use of time and
greater opportunities to connect the curriculum.

Four-Teacher Team

The four-teacher team, Figure 3, is the most commonly used and is the most
logical composition with one teacher specialist in each of the four core areas. It
allows teachers with a single subject certification to teach on the team. The
four teachers may also have one or two additional teaching responsibilities be-

yond the core block to complete their work load. This model utilizes teachers with a strong content preparation in one subject area.

Figure 2

Three-Teacher Team

75-90 Students		
TEACHER A	TEACHER B	TEACHER C
Math	Science	Social Studies
Math	Science	Social Studies
Math	Science	Social Studies
Language Arts	Language Arts	Language Arts
Reading	Reading	Reading

Figure 3

Four-Teacher Team

100-120 Students			
TEACHER A	TEACHER B	TEACHER C	TEACHER D
Math	Science	Language Arts	Social Studies
Math	Science	Language Arts	Social Studies
Math	Science	Language Arts	Social Studies
Math	Science	Language Arts	Social Studies

Four-Teacher Team Across Two Grade Levels

This four-teacher arrangement, Figure 4, combines students across two grade levels. It is used when there is an insufficient number of students to complete a four-teacher single-grade team. While solving a numbers problem, it creates a significant opportunity for a team of teachers to stay with a group of students for two years in a multi-age situation.

Figure 4

Four-Teacher Team Across Grade Levels

50-60 Seventh Grade Students 50-60 Eighth Grade Students			
TEACHER A	TEACHER B	TEACHER C	TEACHER D
Math 7	Science 7	Language Arts 8	Social Studies 8
Math 7	Science 7	Language Arts 8	Social Studies 8
Math 8	Science 8	Language Arts 7	Social Studies 7
Math 8	Science 8	Language Arts 7	Social Studies 7

Four-Teacher Team with a Resource Period

This design, Figure 5, requires core teachers to staff a resource period in addition to teaching four classes. All students and all teachers on the team are scheduled into this resource period. The resource period is extremely flexible because it allows teachers to regroup students for remediation, make-up testing, enrichment, or other activities. It is an excellent design to increase the opportunity to provide for the individual needs of students. Furthermore, it resolves the issue of a teacher assigned to four classes when the normal teaching load is five.

Four-Teacher Team with Encore Courses

In this model, Figure 6, the mathematics, science, social studies, and language arts teachers teach five sections of each subject. During each of the periods, four sections of students are enrolled in courses taught by team members while one group of twenty five students leaves the team to take an encore course. This model allows a team of four teachers to teach five sections of students. The disadvantage is the limitation on the use of flexible scheduling.

Figure 5

Four-Teacher Team with a Resource Period

100-120 Students			
TEACHER A	TEACHER B	TEACHER C	TEACHER D
Math	Science	Language Arts	Social Studies
Math	Science	Language Arts	Social Studies
Math	Science	Language Arts	Social Studies
Math	Science	Language Arts	Social Studies
Resource Period	Resource Period	Resource Period	Resource Period

Figure 6

Four-Teacher Team with Encore Course

125-150 Students				
TEACHER A	TEACHER B	TEACHER C	TEACHER D	ENCORE TEACHERS
Math	Science	Language Arts	Social Studies	Encore Course
Math	Science	Language Arts	Social Studies	Encore Course
Math	Science	Language Arts	Social Studies	Encore Course
Math	Science	Language Arts	Social Studies	Encore Course
Math	Science	Language Arts	Social Studies	Encore Course

Five-Teacher Team

A teaming arrangement of five teachers with 125-150 students can be implemented if a fifth subject such as reading is required for a full year of all students as depicted in Figure 7. While reading and language arts are shown as separate subjects, they could be integrated into a communication course. Having reading as a course on the team can result in greater attention to reading in all remaining core courses.

Figure 7

Five-Teacher Team

125-150 Students				
TEACHER A	TEACHER B	TEACHER C	TEACHER D	TEACHER E
Math	Science	Language Arts	Social Studies	Reading
Math	Science	Language Arts	Social Studies	Reading
Math	Science	Language Arts	Social Studies	Reading
Math	Science	Language Arts	Social Studies	Reading
Math	Science	Language Arts	Social Studies	Reading

Five-Teacher Team with Semester Encore Courses

In some middle schools, no fifth subject is required for an entire year. Under these circumstances, two required semester equivalent courses can be scheduled during the same period in a five-by-five arrangement. In Figure 8, music and physical education are offered on an alternate day basis. The music and physical education teachers are allied with two teams requiring them to meet for common planning on alternate days with both teams. It is an attempt to bring together as parts of one team both core and encore courses.

Five-Teacher Team with Quarter Encore Courses

This arrangement is similar to the five-teacher team with semester courses shown in Figure 8. However, four courses, each nine weeks in length, are combined with the mathematics, science, social studies, and language courses to complete the matrix. Each of four encore courses is rotated through the team for nine weeks. For example, during the first quarter, all students on the team are enrolled in art during the second quarter in technology education, in health during the third quarter, and in family and consumer education in the final quarter. The encore teachers work with four teams to complete the cycle. Figure 9 shows the example of art as the course aligned with the core courses.

Figure 8
Five-Teacher Team with Semester Encore Courses

125-150 Students				
TEACHER A	TEACHER B	TEACHER C	TEACHER D	TEACHER E/F
Math	Science	Language Arts	Social Studies	PE/Music
Math	Science	Language Arts	Social Studies	PE/Music
Math	Science	Language Arts	Social Studies	PE/Music
Math	Science	Language Arts	Social Studies	PE/Music
Math	Science	Language Arts	Social Studies	PE/Music

Figure 9
Five-Teacher Team with Quarter Encore Courses

125-150 Students				
TEACHER A	TEACHER B	TEACHER C	TEACHER D	ENCORE TEACHER
Math	Science	Language Arts	Social Studies	Art
Math	Science	Language Arts	Social Studies	Art
Math	Science	Language Arts	Social Studies	Art
Math	Science	Language Arts	Social Studies	Art
Math	Science	Language Arts	Social Studies	Art

MODELS PLACING ALL TEACHERS ON TEAMS

Interdisciplinary teams, in most middle schools, include language arts, mathematics, social studies, and science. While creating such teams has been a significant step forward, teachers not assigned to teams often feel disenfranchised. They, too, desire to work in small-group settings experiencing the collegial support that comes with teaming. In this section, seven models are presented that place all teachers on teams. The first four attempt to accommodate the core-encore arrangement as described in the preceding section. The last three models organize teams in radically different ways. Since no two middle schools are identical, there is a need for a variety of models to match these programs. Middle school personnel should examine these models and make the necessary adaptations or use the ideas presented to create a new model that fits their particular situation.

Overlapping Core Classes

Figure 10, shows three teams, one at each grade level, with the time of the day when students are scheduled in their core and encore courses. From 11:42 until 1:18, the core classes overlap. With all students in their core classes, the encore teachers can engage in team planning or individual preparation. This model could work in larger schools with two or three teams at one grade level.

Activity Period Schedule

An activity or enrichment period of approximately thirty minutes is included in the daily schedule in a number of middle schools. In the model illustrated in Figure 11, the activity period is scheduled at the end of the day. During this activity period, all students can be assigned to the core teachers on one or more days, providing meeting time for encore teachers. The amount of common planning time available is not equivalent to core teachers' planning time, but it does provide some meeting time for encore teachers within the school day. In a large school with numerous encore teachers, several encore teams should be developed.

Figure 10
Overlapping Core Courses

Sixth Grade Team

8:00	11:42	1:18	2:54
Core		Encore	

Seventh Grade Team

8:00	9:36	11:42	1:18	2:54
Core	Encore	Core		

Eighth Grade Team

8:00	9:36	11:42	1:18	2:54
Encore	Core			

Figure 11
Activity Period Schedule

	Activity Period
Instructional Periods	Encore Planning Time

Core/Encore Teams

In this model, it is assumed that core teachers have six classes, an individual preparation period, and a common planning period. Likewise, encore teachers teach six classes, have an individual preparation period, and are assigned to one of the core teams for planning. In most middle schools, the common planning time for core teams is spread across all periods of the day as shown in Figure 12. When possible, encore teachers should be on teams where they share students with core teachers.

Figure 12

Core/Encore Teams

Period	Team Planning
1	Team 6A
2	Team 6B
3	Team 7A
4	No teams meet
5	Team 7B
6	Team 8A
7	Team 8B
8	No teams meet

Pre-School Planning Period

In most middle schools, teachers have short periods of planning time before and after the instructional class periods as shown in Figure 13. This is in addition to the planning time provided during the school day. In the alternative schedule in Figure 14, time is rearranged to provide all teachers with a common planning period at the beginning of the school day. Note that giving up individual planning time before and after school is compensated by having two individual planning periods during the school day. For example, a teacher's workload in the typical teacher schedule might include five classes, a team planning period and an individual planning period. The teacher's workload in the alternative teacher schedule would include five classes and two individual planning periods along with the common planning time at the beginning of the school day.

The model requires that students report to school twenty minutes later and leave school twenty minutes later than identified in the typical teacher schedule. Creating a common planning time at the end of the school day will not work because of the myriad student activities for which staff members are responsible.

Figure 13

Pre-School Planning Period

Typical Teacher Schedule		Alternative Teacher Schedule	
7:30	Teachers report	7:30	Teachers report
7:30 - 7:50	Individual planning time	7:30 - 8:10	COMMON PLANNING TIME
7:50 - 8:00	Supervision	8:10 - 8:20	Supervision
8:00	Classes begin	8:20	Classes begin
3:00	Classes end	3:20	Classes end
3:00 - 3:10	Supervision	3:20 - 3:30	Supervision
3:10 - 3:30	Individual planning time	3:30	Teachers leave
3:30	Teachers leave		

Possible Schedule of Common Planning Time

Because this model is so powerful with all teachers available for common planning time, a possible schedule of meetings is illustrated in Figure 14. The schedule is designed for a school of 300 students; larger schools could adapt accordingly.

Humanity/Technology Teams

This model "breaks the mold" of current interdisciplinary team scheduling because it places all teachers on teams and all students on two teams – a humanities team and a technology team. It is an attempt to resolve the forced separation of core and encore teams. To explain this model, a sample schedule is provided for a middle school with grades seven and eight. Several parameters of this school are:

Figure 14

Possible Schedule of Common Planning Time

TEAM 1-Sixth Grade Core   TEAM 3-Eighth Grade Core
TEAM 2-Seventh Grade Core   TEAM 4-Encore

WK	DAY	TEAM(S)	PURPOSE OF MEETINGS
1	Mon	1,2,3,4	Teams can meet separately or collectively to share upcoming curricular topics, major tests, projects, assignment dates, or special activities
1	Tue	1,4*	Counselor visits with the sixth grade team and all encore teachers who have these students in class
		2	Discussion of special needs students with special educators
		3	Discussion of curricular issues
			* Encore teachers not involved with the sixth grade meet with team two or three
1	Wed	2,4*	Counselor visits with the seventh grade team and all encore teachers who have these students in class
		3	Discussion of special needs students with special educators
		1	Discussion of curricular issues
1	Thur	3,4*	Counselor visits with the eighth grade team and all encore teachers who have these students in class
		1	Discussion of special needs students with special educators
		2	Discussion of curricular issues
1	Fri	4	Discussion of students with special needs with special educators
		1,2,3	Meeting of core teams to discuss curriculum
2	Mon	1,2,3,4	Professional day for teams or various subgroups
2	Tue	1,2,3,4	Parent calling, conferencing with parents
2	Wed	1,2,3,4	Subgroups on issues such as social activities and recognition and awards
2	Thur	1,2,3,4	Discussion of students by each team
2	Fri	1,2,3,4	Subgroups meet to discuss students, curriculum, etc. depending on need. Team leaders set up this schedule.

1. Grades seven and eight with an enrollment of 120-150 students in each grade.
2. A school day with a minimum of 420 minutes including a 30 minute lunch.
3. Each teacher with 260 minutes of classroom instruction and 130 minutes of team and individual planning time.

The curriculum is divided into two major areas, one labeled technology and the other humanities. In the technology block are four subjects – science, mathematics, technology education, and computer literacy. The humanities block consists of language arts, social studies, reading, art, music, health, foreign language, physical education, and home economics. While the melding of these subject areas into an integrated discipline of technology or humanities may develop, for the present, each subject is identified as a course.

Furthermore, each course is weighted. Mathematics, science, language arts, social studies, and reading receive a full credit; while technology education, computer literacy, art, music, health, foreign language, physical education, and home economics receive one-half credit.

The master schedule, depicted in Figure 15, is set up for all seventh grade students to take their technology block the first 130 minutes of the day. They are taught by a team of two science teachers, two math teachers, one technology education teacher, and one computer teacher. This same team of six teachers provides the technology instruction to eighth grade students the last 130 minutes of the day.

The seventh grade language arts, social studies, and reading teachers meet with art, foreign language, and health teachers for common planning on day one and with music, physical education, and home economics teachers on day two (see Figure 16). In grade eight, the language arts, social studies and reading teachers have common planning time with music, physical education, and home economics teachers on day one and with art, foreign language, and health teachers on day two as shown in Figure 17.

To view the schedule for the technology block, see Figure 18. The entire team of six teachers has periods four through six open for common planning time and individual preparation time.

Courses for one-half credit must be taught on alternate days as opposed to every day for one semester to provide the opportunity for the integration of

Figure 15

Humanity/Technology Teams

Grade Seven

8:00　　　　　　　　10:10　　　　　　　　　　　　　　　　　　　3:00

Technology Math　　　Science Tech Ed　Computer	**Humanities** Language Arts　　　Social Studies　　　Reading Art　　　　　　　　　Home Economics　Music Physical Education　Foreign Language　Health
Technology Math　　　Science Tech Ed　Computer	

Grade Eight

8:00　　　　　　　　　　　　　　　　　　12:50　　　　　3:00

Humanities Language Arts　　　Social Studies　　　Reading Art　　　　　　　　　Home Economics　Music Physical Education　Foreign Language　Health	**Technology** Math　　　Science Tech Ed　Computer
	Technology Math　　　Science Tech Ed　Computer

Figure 16

Humanities Schedule-Grade 7

Periods	1	2	3	4	5	6	7	8	9
Day One Schedule									
Language Arts		Team		7A	7B	7C	7D	7E	7F
Social Studies		and		7B	7C	7D	7E	7F	7A
Reading		Individual		7C	7D	7E	7F	7A	7B
		Planning							
Art		Time		7D	7E	7F	7A	7B	7C
Foreign Language				7E	7F	7A	7B	7C	7D
Health				7F	7A	7B	7C	7D	7E
Day Two Schedule									
Language Arts		Team		7A	7B	7C	7D	7E	7F
Social Studies		and		7B	7C	7D	7E	7F	7A
Reading		Individual		7C	7D	7E	7F	7A	7B
		Planning							
Music		Time		7D	7E	7F	7A	7B	7C
Physical Education				7E	7F	7A	7B	7C	7D
Home Economics				7F	7A	7B	7C	7D	7E

KEY: 7A-7F denotes sections of seventh grade students.

Figure 17
Humanities Schedule-Grade 8

Periods	1	2	3	4	5	6	7	8	9
Day One Schedule									
Language Arts	8A	8B	8C	8D	8E	8F	Team		
Social Studies	8B	8C	8D	8E	8F	8A	and		
Reading	8C	8D	8E	8F	8A	8B	Individual		
							Planning		
Music	8D	8E	8F	8A	8B	8C	Time		
Physical Education	8E	8F	8A	8B	8C	8D			
Home Economics	8F	8A	8B	8C	8D	8E			
Day Two Schedule									
Language Arts	8A	8B	8C	8D	8E	8F	Team		
Social Studies	8B	8C	8D	8E	8F	8A	and		
Reading	8C	8D	8E	8F	8A	8B	Individual		
							Planning		
Art	8D	8E	8F	8A	8B	8C	Time		
Foreign Language	8E	8F	8A	8B	8C	8D			
Health	8F	8A	8B	8C	8D	8E			

Figure 18
Technology Schedule

Periods	1	2	3	4	5	6	7	8	9
	Grade Seven						Grade Eight		
Science	7A	7B	7C	Team and			8A	8B	8C
Math	7B	7C	7A	Individual			8B	8C	8A
Science	7D	7E	7F	Planning			8D	8E	8F
Math	7E	7F	7D	Time			8E	8F	8D
Day One									
Technology Education	7C	7A	7B	Team & Individual			8C	8A	8B
Computer	7F	7D	7E	Planning Time			8F	8D	8E
Day Two									
Technology Education	7F	7D	7E	Team & Individual			8F	8D	8E
Computer	7C	7A	7B	Planning Time			8C	8A	8B

subject matter. As more integration takes place, these lines between class periods will become more blurred. Teachers in both the humanities and technology block have complete control over the block of time assigned to them; time within the block can be scheduled by the teachers. For example, all students in music could come together for band or choral practice for thirty minutes every other day or for longer periods on days just prior to a concert. All classes would be shortened a few minutes to accommodate this need. Students not in band or chorus would be supervised by the remaining teachers in the block and possibly involved in some enrichment activities.

Humanities/Technology Teams with Foreign Language

In order to accommodate foreign languages that are taught in some middle schools, a modification of the previous model is shown. Several conditions are set for this model:

1. The technology block remains the same as in the previous model.
2. Each humanities team has 100-120 students assigned to it.
3. The full-credit subjects on the humanities team are language arts, social studies, Spanish, French, and German. Physical education, music, art and home economics are one-half credit.
4. The language arts and social studies teachers are assigned a "resource class." This is not a study hall but a class that focuses on basic study skills, thinking skills, communication skills, and any other skills that will complement the instructional program. Some silent sustained reading can be included in this class.
5. Students are placed on teams in relation to the language they have selected. The language teachers are shared by all three teams.
6. The French and German teachers are shared with the seventh grade teams. Another Spanish teacher will be needed in grade seven.

Figure 19 depicts the technology schedule which is very similar to the original schedule; Figures 20A, 20B, and 20C show the eighth grade humanities schedule.

Figure 19
Technology Schedule with Foreign Language

Period	1	2	3	4	5	6	7	8	9
	Team 1 - Grade 8						Team 1 - Grade 7		
Science - 1	A	B	C	Team Planning and			S	T	U
Math - 1	B	C	A	Individual Prep			T	U	S
Tech-Ed - 1	C/F	A/D	B/E	"			U/X	S/V	T/W
Comp-Ed - 1	F/C	D/A	E/B	"			X/U	V/S	W/T
Science - 2	D	E	F	"			V	W	X
Math - 2	E	F	D	"			W	X	V
	Team 2 - Grade 8						Team 2 - Grade 7		
Science - 3	G	H	I	Team Planning and			V	Z	AA
Math - 3	H	I	G	Individual Prep			Z	AA	Y
Tech-Ed - 2	I/L	G/J	H/K	"			AA/BB	Y/CC	Z/DD
Comp-Ed - 2	L/I	J/G	K/H	"			BB/AA	CC/Y	DD/Z
Science - 4	J	K	L	"			CC	DD	BB
Math - 4	K	L	J	"			DD	BB	CC
	Team 3 - Grade 8						Team 3 - Grade 7		
Science - 5	M	N	O	Team Planning and			EE	FF	GG
Math - 5	N	O	M	Individual Prep			FF	GG	EE
Tech-Ed - 3	O/R	M/P	N/Q	"			GG/JJ	EE/HH	FF/II
Comp-Ed - 3	R/O	P/M	Q/N	"			JJ/GG	HH/EE	II/FF
Science - 6	P	Q	R	"			HH	II	JJ
Math - 6	Q	R	P	"			II	JJ	HH

Figure 20A
Grade Eight Humanities Schedule - Team One

Period		1	2	3	4	5	6	7	8	9
Every Day										
	Language Arts	Team Planning and					8A	8B	8C	8D
	Social Studies	Individual Prep					8B	8C	8D	8A
	Spanish	Team Planning and			8A	8B				
	French	Individual Prep				8C				
Day One										
	Physical Education	Team Planning and					8C	8D	8A	8B
	Music	Individual Prep					8D	8A	8B	8C
	Study Hall				8D					
	Resource				8C	8D				
	Resource				8B	8A				
Day Two										
	Art	Team Planning and					8C	8D	8A	8B
	Home Economics	Individual Prep					8D	8A	8B	8C
	Study Hall				8D					
	Resource				8B	8D				
	Resource				8C	8A				

Figure 20B

Grade Eight Humanities Schedule - Team Two

Period	1	2	3	4	5	6	7	8	9
Every Day									
Language Arts	Team Planning and			8E	8F			8G	8H
Social Studies	Individual Prep			8F	8G			8H	8E
Spanish	Team Planning and					8E	8F		
French	Individual Prep					8F	8G		
Day One									
Physical Education	Team Planning and			8G	8H			8E	8F
Music	Individual Prep			8H	8E			8F	8G
Resource						8G	8E		
Resource						8H	8H		
Day Two									
Art	Team Planning and			8G	8H			8E	8F
Home Economics	Individual Prep			8H	8E			8F	8G
Resource						8G	8E		
Resource						8H	8H		

Figure 20C

Grade Eight Humanities Schedule - Team Three

Period	1	2	3	4	5	6	7	8	9
Every Day									
Language Arts	Team Planning and			8I	8J	8K	8L		
Social Studies	Individual Prep			8J	8K	8L	8I		
Spanish	Team Planning and							8I	
German	Individual Prep							8J	8K
Day One									
Physical Education	Team Planning and			8K	8L	8I	8J		
Music	Individual Prep			8L	8I	8J	8K		
Study Hall									8L
Resource								8K	
Resource								8L	
Day Two									
Art	Team Planning and			8K	8L	8I	8J		
Home Economics	Individual Prep			8L	8I	8J	8K		
Study Hall									8L
Resource								8K	8I
Resource								8L	8J

Integrated Schedule

This model is designed to integrate more fully the middle school curriculum. Coursework typically found in a middle school is consolidated into four courses. Below are the four courses, showing the disciplines included in each.

Technology	Science, mathematics, computer literacy, technology education
Humanities	Language arts, social studies, reading
Fine Arts	Art, music, drama, speech, foreign language
Wellness	Physical education, health, business education, guidance, family and consumer education

As shown in Figure 21, all periods would be 80-90 minutes. Each of the teams would have one period per day for common planning time and individual preparation and teach three sections of students. At first, the inclination will be to teach "each" of the disciplines included in the four courses. As teachers become more comfortable with the schedule, greater efforts will be made to integrate the disciplines.

Figure 21

Integrated Schedule

Period/Course	1	2	3	4
Technology	A	B	C	Plan
Humanities	B	C	Plan	A
Fine Arts	C	Plan	A	B
Wellness	Plan	A	B	C

Key: A-D indicates a section of approximately 75 students.

SUMMARY

Teams should be designed to support the instructional program of the school. Initial efforts with team designs were almost exclusively restricted to various combinations of the basic academic or core areas. Several slight modifications have been developed to include encore subjects on the core teams but they are relatively rare. The middle school community must not be satisfied with current designs but move ahead and create new ones that include all teachers on teams and thereby release the full potential of teaming. Several models were described to challenge current paradigms of team design. These examples will stimulate others to continue exploring alternative models. Teaming in the middle school is a powerful organizational structure, and models of team designs must be sought that will take advantage of the power of teaming. ❏

3

Organizing and Scheduling Teams

It is difficult to point to a single aspect of a middle school that has as much impact on the children and adults as does the schedule.

– Jeffrey S. Craig

Generating a schedule that accommodates teaming can be difficult and time consuming. Scheduling is dependent on numerous factors which must be considered before the master schedule is developed. In this section, the placement of students and teachers on teams is examined, the variables that affect scheduling are explored, the concept of a master schedule is described, and examples of block scheduling are provided.

PLACEMENT OF TEACHERS AND STUDENTS ON TEAMS

Size of Teams

Generally, the larger the team, the more difficult it is for a team to function effectively. Teams of two to four teachers are most workable. Two-person teams are especially appropriate for students coming from self-contained classrooms with a single teacher. Two- and three-person teams most often need teachers with multiple certification, while larger teams can utilize teachers with single or dual certification. The important thing to recognize about teams with only two or three teachers is the automatic reduction in the number of different students taught and the accompanying increase in the amount of time a teacher and student are together. The reduction in the student-teacher ratio has many inherent and long-term advantages.

The number of encore teachers in a building will vary depending on enrollment, course offering, shared teachers, etc. When encore teams are formed, care must be taken to keep them small to be effective.

Placement of Teachers on Teams

Assigning teachers to teams is one of the principal's most important tasks. Chapter 5 describes various methods for placing teachers on teams and the principal's role in aligning teams. The basic goal, of course, is to develop teams that can work harmoniously and professionally. It is important to note that a team of diverse individuals who can function in a collegial manner will be stronger than a more homogeneous team. With diversity comes a greater range of background experiences and abilities to generate creative ideas for teamwork.

Length of Tenure on Teams

Because it often takes two or three years to become a smoothly functioning unit, changes in team membership should be made only for significant reasons. Unfortunately, in a closed situation such as a middle school, taking a person who is dysfunctional on one team and placing that individual on another team can disrupt the second team. Only after all efforts have been made to correct the problems of the dysfunctional team should a change in team membership be considered. This includes changing team membership where members may get along with one another very well but perform at a low level. Chapter 9 provides more detailed information on dysfunctional teams.

While the principal's evaluation of all teams' performances is ongoing, at the conclusion of each school year definite steps must be taken to help low functioning teams improve. Sometimes this does mean making changes in team membership.

Placement of Students on Teams

When placing students on teams, the overriding consideration is to create a quality learning opportunity for *all* students. Teams should be as close to "equal" as possible with no stigma attached to any team. Those forming teams should consider gender, achievement levels, special needs, and cultural differences. Placing a large number of students with special needs on one team and none on another, for example, creates an imbalance that has significant repercussions on the curriculum offered and the instructional procedures used.

In large schools with three teams at a single grade, it is permissible to place learning-disabled students on one team, emotionally disabled students on another team, and cognitively disabled on the third team. By doing this, all teams have students with special needs, and it is easier to align teachers of special needs students with single teams.

Sectioning of Students

Perhaps the best way to place students on a team into sections is to assign this task to the team members. Allowing them to section students often results in a better mix of individuals than if done by the principal or a computer. Team members should be allowed to move students from one section to another on their team whenever they believe the change is educationally beneficial. Moving students from one team to another is a much more serious decision and should be done only in special situations.

VARIABLES AFFECTING SCHEDULING

Number and Length of Instructional Periods

The time that school activities begin and end obviously determines the number of minutes available for instruction, lunch, and other activities. Middle school personnel usually have little to say about these two points in a day since they hinge on bus schedules and other administrative factors. The total number of minutes available, the length of the lunch period, and the inclusion of an activity period are factors that impact the number of minutes assigned for instructional periods. The more time available for instruction, the greater the number of periods that can be created from this time or the longer times for each period. A study of Wisconsin middle schools, Figure 22, showed a decided preference for the eight period day in order to offer students more opportunities to explore the curriculum (Rottier, Landon, & Rush, 1994).

Advisor-Advisee/Activity Program

Many middle schools set aside 20-30 minutes each day for an advisory and/or student activity program. This block of time can be scheduled at various points during the day. Scheduling the advisory/activity period at the beginning or end of the day increases the number of contiguous instructional periods if block scheduling is desired for teams.

Figure 22

Number of Instructional Periods

Number of periods	Percent of Schools Reporting
6	1
7	22
8	62
9	8
Other	6

Nutrition Breaks

The report, *Turning Points: Preparing American Youth for the 21st Century* (1989) published by the Carnegie Corporation's Council on Adolescent Development, reminds us of the importance of providing for the health and fitness of students in our middle schools. The business world provides workers with breaks to increase their efficiency. This should apply to students as well. Furthermore, in our current society, many students come to school without breakfast or with a breakfast of soda and potato chips. A nutritional break, especially in the morning can assist growing students whose bodies need nourishment. It also provides an opportunity for very legitimate student socialization, and some schools provide for such with no nutrition involved.

Two procedures are used most often to schedule the nutrition or social break. Providing an extended passing time between two classes allows students to mingle at certain places in the building. This procedure requires supervision in the gathering places. Another procedure is to lengthen one class period in mid-morning by ten minutes. Each teacher provides students with break time in his/her classroom and is responsible for their supervision. In middle schools with block scheduling, breaks can be scheduled by the team when appropriate with students remaining in the team area during the break.

Team Meetings

The heart and soul of an interdisciplinary structure is common planning time for the team teachers. During this time, teachers discuss student, instructional, and curricular concerns. A major scheduling issue is the amount of meeting time necessary for a team. The most desirable arrangement is to schedule one period of common planning time each day in addition to an individual preparation period for each teacher. Where this is not possible, the minimum acceptable time for team planning is three periods each week; anything less severely limits the effectiveness of the team. A few middle schools, in their desire to implement teaming, have asked teachers to do their team planning before or after school. This is an invitation to disaster, because such time will slowly dissipate due to conflicts before and after school. It is unwise to ask teachers to substitute team planning time for all their individual planning time. In this situation, individual planning will soon take precedence over team planning. If teams cannot be provided a minimum amount of common planning time during the school day in addition to individual planning time, teaming should not be implemented. Its potential for enhancing curriculum and student achievement is dependent upon adequate team planning time.

Curriculum

The curriculum has a significant impact on the daily schedule. When teaming is implemented, several concerns appear.

- Coursework

  Schools often make curricular changes when they implement teaming. Middle schools need a strong mission statement and definite goals to provide guidance for making curricular decisions. If they do not exist, traditional practices, teacher preferences, and/or the concerns of vocal parents will direct the curricular changes.

- Tracking

  The greater the extent of tracking, the more difficult it is to schedule students. Establishing special classes for certain students reduces the unity so important when establishing teams and interferes with the flexibility provided by a block schedule. The extensive research on tracking ought to be thoroughly analyzed and evaluated. The less tracking, the better. If a middle level school is highly tracked, personnel may wish to implement a long range (3-5 years) detracking goal to minimize the negative effects of tracking on students as well as on scheduling. Schedulers must be cognizant of de facto grouping, especially in smaller schools. Algebra, music, and foreign language may, for example, influence significantly the scheduling of classes for all students.

- Required versus elective courses
  Elective courses have a significant effect on scheduling. When students are allowed to elect courses, the task of those generating the schedule is to place the largest number of students in their top choices. When there is a prescribed curriculum for all students, establishing blocks of time for teams and team planning time are easier to achieve.

- Time allocation for each course
  The amount of time devoted to each course may constitute a major hurdle for schools implementing teaming. The perceived importance of a course is often equated with the amount of time assigned to it; for example, a semester course may be perceived to be twice as valuable as a quarter course. To fit all courses into a schedule that includes team planning time and block scheduling, it may be necessary to consider six-, nine-, twelve-, and eighteen-week courses along with full-year courses.

TEAM DEVELOPMENT AND SCHEDULING

Shared teachers, teacher certification, and teacher workload are items that affect the assignment of teachers to middle school teams and scheduling.

Shared Teachers

In middle schools, especially those in small rural areas, sharing teachers with the high school or an elementary school makes the development of a master schedule with teaming very difficult. If a team of teachers share a common group of students and have a common planning period, they must be assigned to the middle school the same periods of the day. Block scheduling a team demands teacher presence in the building. When teachers must be shared, it is imperative to schedule these teachers into the middle school program first. This may be contrary to existing practices.

A few middle schools, where encore teachers are shared with the high school, have done some creative scheduling so that a block of encore courses are taught to all middle school students at the same time during one period of the day. This procedure allows core teachers to have common planning time while students are with their high school counterparts.

Some middle schools reduce the shared teacher dilemma by hiring teachers with multiple certification. This allows a team of two or three teachers to teach all the subjects, a situation with many advantages. (See Chapter 2 for a description of two- and three-person teams.)

Middle schools with extensive sharing of teachers must establish a long term (3-5 years) goal to reduce or eliminate this practice to improve scheduling of teams. Once this plan is established, personnel and curricular decisions are approved only if the goal of reducing or eliminating shared teachers is advanced.

Teacher Certification

When teams are being organized, the certification of teachers assigned to the middle school will need careful examination. Their certification will play an important role in the development of teams. Where certification hinders team arrangements, schools must establish a plan to match teacher certification with team needs or seek a waiver from the state department.

Some teachers may need to extend their license to include all grades in the middle school or an additional subject field. When the Eau Claire, Wisconsin, school district placed grade six in the middle school, teachers needing grade six added to their license submitted a portfolio of middle level staff development experiences. Working with the University of Wisconsin-Eau Claire, most were able to extend their license without taking additional coursework.

Teacher Work Schedule

The teacher work day requirement has a significant impact on the development and scheduling of teams. In a school with a seven period day, the typical work requirement for a teacher is five classes, one supervisory responsibility, and one individual preparation period. Arrangements in schools with eight period days include five classes, one supervisory responsibility, and two individual preparation periods, or six classes, one supervisory responsibility, and one individual preparation period. Most middle schools have eliminated study halls, thereby reducing the need for that supervisory task. Substituting common planning time for this supervisory activity is a more professional use of teacher time. Teachers not on teams continue their supervisory responsibilities where needed.

The teachers' work schedule most often is negotiated with the school board. Therefore, changes to the existing contract must be discussed with the teacher organization and the school board.

DEVELOPING THE MASTER SCHEDULE

For teachers to have common planning time, their students must be involved in other classes during team planning. A master schedule indicating how this is accomplished is shown in Figure 23. For grade six, the students take their encore classes during periods one and two and their core classes during the remaining periods. Since the same teachers who teach the encore classes in grade six teach these courses to seventh and eighth graders, the encore classes for grade seven occur later during periods three and four and in grade eight during periods six and seven. This allows the core teachers in each grade to meet as a team when their students are in encore classes. If there is more than one core team in a grade, the schedule below could be adapted to use with one grade.

Figure 23

Master Schedule

Period	1	2	3	4	5	6	7
6th Grade	Encore		Core				
7th Grade	Core		Encore		Core		
8th Grade	Core					Encore	

During the time that a core team's students are in the encore classes, the core teachers have their individual and team planning time as depicted in Figure 24. Note that during period five, all students are in the core classes allowing time for the encore teachers to meet as a team. (See Chapter 2 for a more detailed explanation of common planning time for encore teachers.)

Figure 24

Core Teacher Schedule

Period	1	2	3	4	5	6	7
6th Grade	Team	Prep	Core				
7th Grade	Core		Team	Prep	Core		
8th Grade	Core					Team	Prep

BLOCK SCHEDULING

Block scheduling provides a team of teachers contiguous instructional periods during the school day. Because students are not scheduled for courses other than those taught by team members, the team has complete control of the time allocated to them.

Use of this block of time is limited only by the creativity and initiative of the team. On opposite ends of the continuum on how the block is used are the assignment of equal periods of time for each discipline on the team and a field trip for the entire block of time wherein all students and all team members participate. Between these two extremes are innumerable possibilities for the team. The team can utilize the "pep-rally" schedule, often used in the high school, where a small amount of time is subtracted from each class period to create a period of time in which all students and all teachers are free of class. This time can be used to have team assemblies, videos, speakers, award programs, talent shows, or for giving a test to all students in one subject area. It offers tremendous opportunities to work with small groups of students on the team. For example, if several students did poorly on an exam, one teacher could meet with those students for reteaching while the remaining students are under the jurisdiction of the other teachers. Or, one teacher might offer a group of interested students the opportunity to engage in a unique and challenging activity.

The seventh grade interdisciplinary team from Lyons Middle School in Clinton, Iowa, created numerous arrangements to make time fit the instructional needs of the team. Several of their schedules are depicted below.

Normal Schedule

Figure 25 shows the normal schedule for the Lyons Middle School day. The students are involved in encore classes during the time preceding 10:20 a.m. while their teachers are either planning as a team or engaged in individual preparation. When students come to the area of the building to start their core block, a sign in the hallway indicates the location they are to go to at 10:20. At this point, they receive the schedule for the remainder of the day.

Figure 25

Normal Schedule

Time	Activity
8:00-10:20	Encore
10:20-11:05	Class
11:05-11:35	Lunch
11:35-12:20	Class
12:20-1:05	Class
1:05-1:25	Homeroom
1:25-2:10	Class
2:10-2:55	Class
2:55-3:17	Homeroom

Research and Reteaching

If all students are working on research projects, this schedule allows them to come together at one time either in the library or some other location to utilize the project materials. This arrangement is also useful for reteaching a topic to a particular group of students. For example, if fifteen students did not show sufficient mastery on a test in one of the team courses, then during the 10:20-11:20 period, (Figure 26), those fifteen students meet with a team member for a reteaching session while all remaining students are involved in an enrichment or other appropriate activity under the jurisdiction of the other teachers on the team.

Figure 26

Research and Re-teaching Schedule

Time	Activity
8:00-10:20	Encore
10:20-11:20	Research/Reteaching
11:20-11:50	Lunch
11:50-12:30	Class
12:30-1:10	Class
1:10-1:50	Homeroom
1:50-2:30	Class
2:30-3:17	Class

Computer Resource Schedule

Often, the computer facility is not available during the entire day for classes of students. The schedule in Figure 27 allows the team to interchange class periods so all student have the opportunity to use the computer resources.

Assembly/Video/Test Schedule

On some occasions, it is desirable to bring all students together for an assembly, to show a video, or to have students take a test. The assembly/video/test schedule in Figure 28 allows time at the end of the day for these activities to take place. The special event could be scheduled any period within the block of time.

These examples indicate a few of the many schedules that are possible when a team has control over the time for their classes. The block schedule provides almost unlimited opportunities for the team to creatively match time to the goals of instruction.

Figure 27

Computer Schedule

Time	Activity
8:00-10:20	Encore
10:20-11:15	Class
11:15-11:45	Lunch
11:45-12:30	Class
12:30-1:15	Class (Computers)
1:15-2:00	Class
2:00-2:45	Class
2:45-3:17	Homeroom

Figure 28

Assembly/Video/Test Schedule

Time	Activity
8:00-10:20	Encore
10:20-11:15	Class
11:15-11:45	Lunch
11:45-12:30	Class
12:30-1:15	Class
1:15-2:00	Class
2:00-2:45	Class
2:45-3:17	Assembly/Film/Test

SUMMARY

Many new variables occur when middle schools implement teaming. Scheduling is an extremely important task because it places students, teachers, and the curriculum in contact with one another for the purpose of quality teaching and learning. Principals and teachers responsible for scheduling must approach the task in a very enlightened, thoughtful, and careful manner. Developing the master schedule is not just an administrative task. It should reflect the commitment to the middle school philosophy and goals. The greater the commitment, the more time and energy will be spent in this endeavor, and a more productive master schedule will result. ❑

4

The Team Leader

*A successful leader has to be innovative. If you're
not one step ahead of the crowd you'll soon be a
step behind everyone else.*

          – Coach Tom Landry

Too little attention has been paid to the role of the team leader in an interdisciplinary organization. The role of department chairperson has been long established with its primary focus on carrying out routine duties including ordering supplies and materials and assisting with the development of the department budget. Seldom were department chairpersons expected to provide real leadership in student development, curriculum development, or instructional improvement.

In many middle schools where teams exist, the role of the team leader is unclear. To assure that no one would get "stuck" doing whatever the team leader was supposed to do, often the role was rotated among members each year, semester, or quarter. However, it is increasingly clear that leadership is so critical, it requires careful examination.

In a study of middle schools by George and Shewey (1994), eighty-one percent of the respondents indicated that team leaders play an important role and have contributed to the long-term effectiveness of the middle school program.

This chapter elaborates on the numerous roles that team leaders play, the procedures used to select team leaders and placement on teams, length of appointment and remuneration, and the professional growth of team leaders.

ROLE OF THE TEAM LEADER

The roles of the team leader are many and include the six major responsibilities described in the following pages.

Selection of New Team Members

Traditionally, the principal made all decisions involved in the hiring of teachers. This was logical because each teacher reported directly to the principal. In a school with a teaming arrangement, however, it is the team leader who is in constant contact with staff members on the team. To ensure a harmonious relationship on the team and with the administration, the team leader ought to play a key role in selecting new players on the team.

The team leader, and often the entire team, should be involved in early discussions about replacing a team member and in writing the job description. Perusing credentials of applicants to select those persons who will be invited for interviews should be done in cooperation with the principal. All team members should be involved in the interview process. The formal selection of the person to be hired is done by the principal, but, having the team leader involved in all facets of hiring strengthens the importance of the team within the middle school.

Providing Assistance to New Team Members

Team leaders must have a constant concern for the professional development of the team members. Teaming provides a superb induction program for teachers new to the school, especially if the new teacher is just making the transition from college to the classroom. In a nurturing environment, neophytes can gain a sense of pride and confidence in their role as team members.

The team leader must work with all members of the team to help them perform at the top of their ability. While new teachers are quite willing and pleased to be assisted by the team leader, more experienced teachers may not be as willing. Thus the team leader needs to possess the leadership skills to interact successfully with all team personnel.

Developing Curriculum

Teaming offers a small group of teachers enormous opportunities to shape the curriculum for the benefit of their students. Meeting on a daily basis provides team members with ample opportunities to learn about one another's curriculum and how to connect their subject areas. Team leaders can play a key role in focusing discussion on improving the curriculum for students. If the team leader is committed to the concept of curriculum integration, this enthusiasm will be recognized by team members and can go a long way toward assisting in this endeavor. The team leader must recognize opportunities for integration and be willing to bring this information to the attention of team members.

Managing Student Behavior

Teaming presents ample opportunities for achieving consistency among teachers in the management of student behavior. Helping team members develop common requirements in conjunction with their students and then encouraging consistency in applying these procedures is an important function of the team leader. Team discussions on behavior initiated by the team leader will help beginning teachers and those weak in classroom management skills gain confidence in this area.

Meeting the Social Needs of Students

Team leaders need to ensure that an appropriate amount of team planning time is devoted to ways of meeting the social and emotional needs of students.

Collective discussion of the particular needs of students can result in various ways of meeting their social needs, including groupwork, class parties, socials, and field trips.

Managing Resources

This role is similar to that held by department chairpersons. Team leaders assist teams in acquiring the resources necessary to meet instructional responsibilities and managing those resources in a prudent manner.

Communicating

A major role of the team leader is establishing good communication within the team and between the team and other constituencies in the school, including the principal, faculty, other teams, guidance counselors, nurse, parents, and the students themselves. This is done orally through a team liaison person and in written form through letters, notes, team meeting minutes, and team publications.

A TEAM LEADER'S JOB DESCRIPTION

An example of a team leader's job description is the following from the Bonduel (Wisconsin) Middle School.

General Responsibility of the Team Leader
- To promote the middle school philosophy and to provide leadership in the planning, coordinating, implementing, and evaluating of the middle school program and curriculum

Specific Responsibilities of the Team Leader
- Provide leadership in establishing team goals for the year
- Preside over team meetings

- Use consensus in reaching decisions where appropriate
- Facilitate discussion of individual student academic and behavioral progress
- Involve all team members in discussions and meetings
- Encourage open and honest communication in sharing ideas
- Facilitate the integration of course content and skills on a regular basis; coordinate the development of interdisciplinary teaching units
- Assist the team in assessing progress toward the goals; facilitate the completion of the annual team assessment document
- Coordinate all parent/team conferences
- Establish and maintain an accurate student file system which includes parental contacts, interventions tried, counselor referrals, etc.
- Represent the best interests of the entire team at team leader/principal meetings
- Assist in the selection of new personnel
- Attend yearly team leader inservice meeting

This example illustrates well the range of a team leader's duties and should help communicate the breadth of the role.

DESIGNATING TEAM LEADERS

Team members may become team leaders through rotation, selection by team members, or administrative appointment.

Rotation

This procedure is used when no one person desires to be the team leader and the role has been ill-defined. Rotational team leadership is based on the assumption that the team leader is expected to assume a variety of responsibilities that no one wants to do for an entire year; therefore, it is passed around to each team member. This plan is obviously flawed in many ways. First, the team leader should not be expected to play all the roles involved in a team, leader, recorder, liaison, etc. Every member of the team needs to assume one or more roles. Second, not every teacher possesses the skills or the desire to be a team leader. Many teachers are excellent team members but experience frustration when asked to lead the team. Third, the role of the team leader is far too important to be handled in a happenstance manner. A key to the effectiveness of every team is how well the team leader exercises leadership in assisting the team in fulfilling its respon-

sibilities. Rotational service does not bode well for the development of effective teams.

Selection by Team Members

While seeming like a very democratic procedure, selection by vote of the team members has the potential to be ineffective. Sometimes such a selection is based on popularity, experience, or

because a particular person has an ax to grind and other team members feel they should or should not allow this individual to be the leader. Furthermore, there may be no one person on the team that desires to be a team leader or is willing to accept this responsibility. If we believe that team leaders can have a significant influence on the actions of the team, this method of selecting a team leader may not place the best person in this important role.

Appointment by the Principal

Having the team leaders appointed by the principal is the most logical and appropriate method of making this decision. The principal may invite potential candidates for a team leader position to discuss the possibility and/or to apply. If the principal believes that certain individuals have great potential to be team leaders, these people should be encouraged to apply. Once those willing and able have been determined, the principal can proceed with interviews and make

assignments that will have the greatest positive effect on the various teams.

It is important for the principal to match the qualities of the team leader with the particular nature of the team. If a team is just beginning to work with the concept of teaming, a team leader that can provide direction is especially important. If a team has been having difficulties, then a person who can play a strong supportive role would be the best choice. In all cases, the principal must accept the selection and placement of team leaders as an extremely important responsibility.

TENURE, REMUNERATION, AND GROWTH OF TEAM LEADERS

Tenure

While each situation is distinctive, as a general rule, it is wise for a team leader to be appointed for a period of three years. The first year will be a professional growth experience. To reassign after one year means that year's experience is lost. It is also advisable to have an ending date for the assignment of team leaders. First, it gives the team leader an opportunity to make a gracious exit from the position after providing a term of service. Second, if the team leader is doing only a mediocre job, it allows the principal to make a change rather easily. Third, this procedure opens the way for other teachers to prepare for and accept the challenge of being a team leader.

The principal should formally evaluate each team leader annually. These assessments should be viewed as an opportunity for team leaders to reflect on their effectiveness and, with the help of the principal, to grow in their abilities as team leaders. Certainly, a change in team leadership can and should be made earlier than three years when circumstances warrant a change.

Remuneration

The remuneration of team leaders, if any, will depend on many factors. Precedent, union contracts, and local budgets are among factors that determine how team leaders are rewarded. If the job description for a team leader requires work outside the school day, then in most middle schools this qualifies the person occupying this position for some remuneration. If it does not require outside activities, then perhaps no remuneration is required. Remuneration can be in the form of a stipend, released time, or extra perks. Released time from a supervision duty may be seen by some team leaders as more valuable than a stipend. Providing team leaders with financial support to attend conferences and workshops is an excellent way to reward these individuals for their efforts. Or, some combination of stipend, released time, and perks can be arranged. At any rate, the position of team leader is enhanced if some identifiable benefit is attached to it.

Professional Growth of Team Leaders

All too few opportunities have been provided for team leaders to grow professionally by attending workshops geared specifically to improve their knowledge and skills. Some team leader training may be available from technical colleges that offer training for personnel in the business world. If this type of staff development is not available, the principal should facilitate

some in-house staff development for team leaders. Since the effectiveness of a team hinges on the capabilities of the team leader, it is important that the principal arranges staff development opportunities for team leaders through local activities, conferences, or at the least through professional reading.

SUMMARY

Although teams have become an integral component of middle schools, the role of the team leader has been undervalued. If middle schools are looking for ways to improve teaming, a significant place to start is with the team leader position. The position is unique because the person in the role of team leader is a full-time faculty member and a colleague of the remaining members of the team. This uniqueness should not deter middle schools from strengthening this position through appropriate selection, assignment, and professional growth of team leaders. ❑

5

The Principal's Role in Teaming

Enlightened leaders know how to get their people
excited about their mission.

– Ed Oakley and Doug Krug

The principal plays a pivotal role in the development and implementation of teaming. Teaming calls for a fundamental change in the organizational structure. Instead of teachers reporting directly to the principal, in a teaming structure the principal interacts with teams as an entity and with individual teachers through the team leader. The change in structure brings concomitant changes in the role of the principal.

Principals must have a thorough understanding of and a belief in the interdisciplinary organization. The attitudes and actions of the principal can enhance or hinder the operation of teams both in schools where teaming is being initiated and in those schools with a history of teaming.

This chapter covers selecting and placing teachers on teams, monitoring and assisting teams, working with team leaders, and solving team problems.

SELECTING AND PLACING TEACHERS ON TEAMS

Assigning teachers to teams is a critical responsibility of the principal when teaming is implemented. Effective teams consist of teachers who are able to work harmoniously and creatively for the benefit of their students. Special care must be taken to ensure this harmony when the principal makes team assignments.

There are two basic ways to organize teams: have the principal assign teachers to teams, or have the principal collaborate with team leaders in making the placements. When the first strategy is used, the principal runs the risk of having insufficient knowledge of individuals who can work together in a collegial manner. Team leaders are generally in an advantageous position to know the nuances of individual teachers. It may be valuable to ask each teacher, in a confidential manner, if there are any teachers with whom they would have difficulty working. This information can provide additional insights for the principal and team leaders as teachers are assigned to teams. If team leaders are appointed before teachers are assigned to teams, the collaboration of principal and team leaders is the preferred means of placing teachers on teams.

Except in very special circumstances, teachers should not select their teammates. This procedure has the potential to create super teams and very poor teams that ultimately affect students assigned to them. Furthermore, if a few teachers are not well liked by the majority of teachers, this self-selection process can exacerbate the situation.

When hiring new teachers, it is important to select people who will "fit" the team to which they are assigned The credentials of candidates should be examined carefully to help determine if they have the potential to be a team player. Perhaps the candidate was a member of a successful team in another school or belonged to an athletic team or forensics team at a university. During student teaching, the individual may have been placed in a school with a teacher on a team. Experiences like these generally indicate that a person is likely to mesh with the team to which the individual is assigned.

Team members should be involved in interviewing each of the candidates for the opening on their team. This is a great opportunity to involve teachers in crucial decision-making. Furthermore, it places a stamp of importance on the concept of teaming in the school.

ALIGNING TEAM LEADERS AND TEAMS

When aligning team leaders and teams, the reactions of team members to the proposed team leader must be considered along with the potential of the person to lead the team. A team composed of inexperienced team members will benefit from a team leader capable of providing direction and supervision. An experienced team that is functioning at a high level is better served by a team leader capable of support and delegation. An appropriate match between team leader and team is crucial to the effectiveness of the team. Chapter 4 explores the characteristics and responsibilities of team leaders.

MONITORING TEAM PERFORMANCE

The responsibilities of the principal continue after teams and team leaders have been selected. To ensure proper functioning, it is imperative that the principal monitor the progress of teams. There are several procedures that a principal can use.

The principal can manage by wandering around, to borrow a phrase popular in the business world. This implies principals leave their offices and become aware of all that is happening in the building simply by being present in classrooms, team meetings, and hallways. Bulletin boards, murals, and hallway decorations are evidence of team endeavors. Talking to students can determine their perceptions of how things are going on the team. By visiting team meetings, the principal can determine how effectively they are being conducted; however, principals must be aware that their presence at team meetings can change the nature of the meetings. Requiring team leaders to submit a weekly report on the activities of the team is another

means of monitoring progress. Returning these reports with comments will strengthen the communication between principal and teams. Finally, meeting regularly with the team leaders builds a communication network between administration and teams, and among teams, and serves as a support group for the team leaders.

NURTURING TEAMS

While the team leader is responsible for providing direction to the team at each stage of development, the principal must provide team leaders with the assistance and support they need to carry out their responsibilities. The principal should provide overt commendations to those teams that are achieving their goals and working harmoniously through notes to teams, positive oral statements in staff meetings, and comments about team efforts in communications that go to parents.

Besides providing positive feedback to teams that are functioning well, the principal also has the more difficult task of nurturing teams having difficulties. It is important, of course, that the principal allow team leaders and teams an opportunity to resolve their own problems before becoming involved. The principal provides direction and support to the team leaders as they work through problems their teams are encountering before making any direct intervention in team affairs.

SUMMARY

Several benefits accrue to principals as a result of organizing the faculty into teams. The research of Paul George and Kathy Shewey (1994) and others reveals that discipline problems are reduced, and teachers' sense of efficacy increases with no loss in achievement on traditional tests reported. These changes assist the principal in fulfilling more of a leadership role rather than one of a manager. Newer responsibilities come with teaming. They include understanding the philosophy of teaming, how effective teams function, early warning signs of dysfunctional teams, and steps to take when a team is having difficulties. Principals must engage in personal professional staff development to accomplish effectively the tasks before them. ❑

6

Developing Effective Teams

The essence of synergy is to value the differences,
to respect them, to build on strengths.

– Stephen Covey

Teacher preparation programs in the past have focused on helping each person become the best possible teacher in the individual classroom. Few efforts were made to encourage or prepare prospective teachers to work with one another. Effective teams do not result, however, from placing several people trained to work independently on a team, and, then charging them with a set of expectations that require collaboration.

This chapter will focus on the characteristics of effective teams including setting team goals, defining roles of team members, and establishing basic ground rules for effective team meetings. The stages that groups go through on their way to becoming high performance teams are also discussed.

TEAM GOALS

The most effective teams have clear goals and a commitment to work toward those goals. Each year, near the close of the spring semester, interdisciplinary teams should assess their current goals and establish new ones for the following year. Goals will likely involve curriculum, instruction, and assessment; they may focus on the social and emotional behaviors of students, improving communication, developing a positive climate, and/or connecting with parents.

Typical Team Goals
Following are some typical goals for interdisciplinary teams.
- Design and teach a designated number of thematic units, some based on student interests and concerns

- Plan social activities and field trips for students
- Make greater use of the flexibility available with the block schedule
- Meet with all the parents of students on the team
- Improve the communication with encore teachers
- Continue the development of a positive climate
- Make greater use of technology in the instructional program
- Involve encore teachers in team activities
- Involve the team in a service learning project

An examination of these goals indicates they are written for the teachers. Furthermore, it is often difficult to determine if a team has successfully met such general goals.

New Goals

While the goals above are desirable ones, teams will increase their effectiveness by refocusing the emphasis away from what the teachers do and move toward identifying the direct impact on students. Goals should be challenging, explicit, and measurable, thereby providing specific direction to the team. Furthermore, they must identify criteria by which the team can determine if its objectives have been met. Below is a list of goals that focus on students and provide explicit direction for teams. Writing the goals with "...at least _____ percent" encourages the team to go beyond the stated criterion.

- Increase the average daily attendance of students by at least _____ percent
- Increase parent attendance at conferences by at least _____ percent
- Increase the participation of students in clubs and activities by at least _____ percent
- Decrease missing assignments by at least _____ percent
- Decrease discipline referrals to the office by at least _____ percent
- Decrease incidents of disruptive behavior outside the team by at least _____ percent

- Increase parent involvement in school activities by at least _____ percent
- Decrease gender imbalance in student activities by at least _____ percent
- Increase student involvement in team social activities by at least _____ percent
- Increase student achievement on the state mathematics test by at least _____ percent
- Increase student achievement on the persuasive writing portion of the state English test by least _____ percent
- Increase student opportunities to connect with adults in the building by at least _____ percent
- Increase the number of students who begin class having eaten a healthy breakfast by at least _____ percent
- Increase student attendance at school events, involvement in the science fair, color day, etc. by at least _____ percent
- Increase the number of students who use peer mediation by at least _____ percent
- Decrease drug and alcohol referrals by at least _____ percent
- Decrease tardiness to school by at least _____ percent

Teams are encouraged to consider establishing additional goals using these as examples to stimulate their thinking.

Selecting and Assessing Goals

Teams must give careful consideration to the selection of goals and decide how they can meet them. Once selected, the team should examine curriculum, teaching strategies, climate, and all other facets of their program that impact the goals. Plans to implement, monitor, and assess the goals must be established at the time they are selected. Chapter 9 provides some tools for collecting and analyzing data.

Selecting measurable goals carries with it a risk of failure. However, not reaching an established goal can be a valuable learning experience. When analyzing the data collected on a goal, it is important to determine why the goal was not reached and what might be done to achieve it in the future.

The task of collecting and portraying data for the assessment of a goal could be done by the mathematics teacher with the help of students on the team. The mathematics teacher could obtain the data and use them in a learning activity with students. Results in the form of student-generated charts and graphs might be displayed in the team area to inform and motivate students. Many of the goals stated above could be handled in a similar fashion, that is, involving students in the data collection and reporting of the results. Furthermore, some goals lend themselves to classroom discussions that will lead to improved student performance.

TEAM ROLES

Having each teacher on the team assume one or more of the team responsibilities is an excellent means of building team unity and interdependence. In addition, dividing the workload is the only way all team responsibilities can be accomplished. Examples of various roles and responsibilities follow.

Role	Responsibility
Leader	Provides leadership. (See Chapter 4 for a detailed explanation of the team leader role.)
Recorder	Keeps a record of actions and decisions made by the team and serves as the team historian.
Team Liaison	Communicates with the administration, other teams, encore teachers, support staff, and others to obtain or share information.
Gatekeeper	Provides feedback to members of the team, especially when there are dysfunctional behaviors evident. (Examples include dominating, withdrawing, and antagonizing behaviors.) May also serve as timekeeper.
Resource Person	Obtains and manages resources needed to implement team activities.
Public Relations	Keeps people informed about the many activities and accomplishments of the students and faculty on the team; prepares news stories.
Social Activities	Organizes social activities for students and teachers on the team.

The three roles of leader, recorder, and liaison are essential. Other roles with concomitant expectations including ones not mentioned here can be established at the discretion of the team.

The nature of the responsibilities of the team leader makes it advisable that that person should be appointed for three years; all other roles can be changed each year or more frequently. It is important that role assignments not be done on a seniority basis or any other system that prevents all members from full participation on the team. To create a sense of belonging on a team, each team member should be responsible for at least one ongoing responsibility.

TEAM RECORDS

The maintenance of complete team records is imperative. These records make it possible to trace team activities and decisions. Of specific importance are records of discussions and actions on behalf of students. These records will be important when conferring with parents or recommending major changes in a student's program. In addition, an accurate record of team activities will be invaluable if critics of teaming seek to reduce or eliminate common planning time.

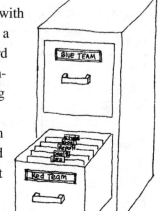

Recordkeeping can be simplified by using a form such as the one portrayed in Figure 29. A standard form will help to ensure the recording of pertinent information on all team activities.

GROUND RULES

Every team must establish rules to govern its operation. Known as ground rules, they help each member display the behaviors necessary to make teaming function smoothly. A number of suggested ground rules follow.

Meeting Time

Common planning time takes place within the confines of a regularly sched-uled period. Since a majority of schools have class periods of 40-50 minutes, it

Figure 29

Recordkeeping Form

Item	Team Action	Person Responsible	Target Date

Team Name: Date: _____
Members Present:
Guests: _____

is important to maximize the use of limited time. Teams must establish a precise starting and ending time. For example, if the period begins at 10:03, the team could establish 10:06 as the time to begin the meeting. If the class period ends at 10:45, the team might declare 10:42 as the ending time in order to return to their classrooms for the next class. In this example, there are exactly 36 minutes of meeting time. If one person is five minutes late, the meeting time is reduced by 14 percent. An effective team cannot conduct business without all members present for the entire meeting.

Attendance

Attendance at team meetings is as mandatory as being in class to conduct teaching responsibilities. Other than an emergency, the only reason to be absent from a team meeting is being legally absent from school. Skipping meetings to do other work must be treated as a very serious breech of contract. The principal must establish this requirement when teaming is first introduced and occasionally remind all faculty of this requirement. The principal supports this mandate by not scheduling activities that interfere with team meetings. District-wide activities such as curriculum writing should be scheduled to minimize the number of times team members will be absent. Lack of attendance or tardiness to team meetings is an obvious symptom of a dysfunctional team.

Meeting Place

The team meeting location should be consistent so team members do not question its whereabouts each day. The best meeting place is one devoted solely to team meetings where external stimuli are not present as they may be when meetings are held in a classroom. The room should be equipped with a large table, comfortable chairs, one or more filing cabinets, a writing board, and a bulletin board.

Having a place devoted solely or primarily to team planning sets a positive climate for meetings. It sends a strong message about the importance of common planning time. New middle schools should include a team work room/office/meeting area for each team located in the pod or area of the flexible classrooms.

Interruptions

When teams are planning, personnel in the building often interrupt them to communicate with one or more team members. Team members may unconsciously be encouraging these interruptions by allowing people to come into the meeting with no advance warning. Teams must establish the importance of the meetings and convey this message to others in the building. The team might place the following sign on the door: "Team Meeting in Progress: Please Do Not Disturb." Initially this may be viewed as rude, but personnel in the school will soon respect the desire to conduct effective team meetings. Anyone desiring to speak to the team during team planning time should contact the team leader and be placed on the agenda of an upcoming meeting or catch team members before or after the formal meeting.

Interpersonal Behaviors

A survey of teachers about the interpersonal behaviors and characteristics necessary for members of effective teams resulted in this list:

student centered	trustworthy
respectful	honest
team player	sense of humor
listener	professional
cooperative	patient
consistent	positive
committed to the team	supportive

During staff development prior to teaming (see Chapter 7), these items should be discussed. When determining team goals, members could select one or more of these interpersonal behaviors to pursue. The team should discuss ways of helping members acquire and display these characteristics and conduct an assessment each quarter to determine progress on these goals.

Participation/Discussion Rules

To ensure full participation of everyone in the meetings, team members should agree on a number of basic procedures. Below are some rules which might be adopted by a team.

- Everyone contributes equally
- Each person must indicate her/his true feelings before decisions are made
- Members speak freely on any topic without criticism
- All listen attentively and openly to ideas expressed
- All listen courteously, recognizing the power of nonverbal behaviors
- Everyone is able to express a viewpoint without being interrupted
- Members stay focused on the topic under discussion

- Members will refrain from side conversations
- Members will not correct papers or engage in other personal activities

Ground rules should be established and reviewed each year. When team composition changes, they must be reexamined. Once in place, ground rules should be posted in the team meeting room as a reminder of team expectations.

STAGES OF TEAM DEVELOPMENT

All successful teams, whether in professional sports, business, or education, go through a series of predictable stages from the initial gathering of group members to reaching a high performance level. Intertwined in these stages are distinct feelings and behaviors of the individuals relative to the concept of teaming. Many authors discuss stages of team development with special recognition given to the work of Bruce W. Tuckman (1965).

Being aware of these stages is of significance to the team leader as this person guides the journey of the team. By reflecting and reacting to the feelings and behaviors of individuals on the team, team leaders can provide the type of leadership necessary to move expeditiously to higher performance levels.

Stage One

In this initial stage, a group of individuals comes together in the quest to function as a team. While most individuals have positive feelings about the group's potential to achieve certain tasks, some may be ambivalent or even hostile to the team concept. Group members may have a general idea where their journey will take them but often are confused about how the group can achieve its goals. The productivity level of a team in Stage One is minimal.

The team leader plays a key role during this initial stage. Members will look to the leader for guidance. If it is not provided, then confusion, suspicion, and anxiety will prevail. Leaders serve their teams best by providing direction in establishing goals, helping members sort out various roles, and developing a set of ground rules for team meetings.

Stage Two

Stage Two is sometimes characterized as the political or power stage. Some members of the team will exert considerable influence on the team while others withdraw. Personal agendas may abound. Ground rules will be tested. Often the morale of the team is quite low. This happens when a group of people realize the efforts and sacrifices necessary to function as a team while not possessing the skill level needed to accomplish these tasks. Depending on the extent of the arguing, bickering, and other types of negative behaviors, the productivity level may not increase very significantly.

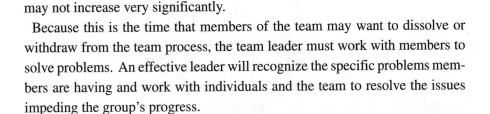

Because this is the time that members of the team may want to dissolve or withdraw from the team process, the team leader must work with members to solve problems. An effective leader will recognize the specific problems members are having and work with individuals and the team to resolve the issues impeding the group's progress.

Stage Three

If individuals on the team are able to recognize problems they are having, and, if there is a belief that by working together the team can overcome these problems, the team will move to a new stage. Team members begin to recognize the strengths that each team member brings to the team and capitalize on these strengths. They become more comfortable working within the established ground rules and start to enjoy one another's presence. Often, they share personal situations. They provide support for one

another. Teams in Stage Three have greater skill in solving problems and making decisions, resulting in greater productivity, satisfaction, and pride for team members.

The team leader supports the efforts of the team by providing positive feedback and recognition of accomplishments.

Stage Four

This is the goal of any team – to reach a high level of productivity and personal satisfaction with teaming. A team in Stage Four finds it relatively easy to make decisions and solve problems. Members adhere to ground rules. They become reflective about the progress of the team, seeking ways to keep the team performing at a high level. In a sense, all members of the team exert leadership with the team leader playing the role of facilitator and coordinator.

It is difficult for a team to function continuously at this level; occasionally, they will drop back to Stage Three, but the nature of the team members is such that they will strive to regain their high performance level.

The speed at which a group of people can move from the gathering stage to one of high performance will depend on a number of variables. The desire to function as a team held by team members greatly influences movement through these stages. The skill of the team leader in providing direction and assistance will enhance the journey. A quality staff development program that develops a knowledge base and the skills of teaming can ensure a proper start and continued success with teaming.

SUMMARY

When teams are formed, they face *task* issues and *people* issues. Task issues include setting goals, establishing roles, and developing decision-making, problem-solving, and conflict-resolving procedures. Setting ground rules such as meeting times, attendance, and discussion/participation rules to govern team behaviors comprise the people issues. Staff development provides opportunities to understand the issues and generate guidelines for effective operation. Furthermore, teams learn that high performance develops in stages. Being aware of these stages will help teams progress with a minimum of frustration and dissatisfaction. ❏

7

Staff Development for Teaming

*The single distinguishing characteristic of
the best professionals in any field is that they
consistently strive for better results, and are
always learning to be more effective, from
whatever source they can find.*

– Michael Fullan and Andy Hargreaves

Too many middle schools implement teaming with little or no preparation. Without appropriate staff development dealing with this powerful organizational strategy, teachers, team leaders, and principals are likely to become frustrated and students will realize few benefits from teaming.

This chapter presents staff development ideas for middle school teachers and administrators who are considering teaming. Five levels or steps of staff development are described: initial staff development, visits to quality middle schools, team leader development, team building, and establishing consistent expectations for students on teams. Finally, team meeting activities are outlined and a potential schedule of these activities is presented.

STEP ONE: INITIAL STAFF DEVELOPMENT

Initial staff development activities lead to an understanding of an interdisciplinary organization and its possibilities for enhancing students, staff, and the curriculum. Developing responses to the following questions will help gain this needed understanding of teaming.

- What is meant by interdisciplinary teaming? How does this differ from previous attempts at team teaching?
- What possibilities does teaming create for students? for staff members? for parents? for administrators? for the curriculum?

- How are teams organized? Who designs the teams? What factors should be considered in designing teams?
- How are students assigned to teams? How are students assigned to sections within a team?
- What happens when team members do not get along with one another? What if they want to change teams?
- How do special education teachers relate to teams? Are they assigned to teams? How often do they meet with teams? How are their students assigned to teams?
- What is the role of the team leader? Who selects the team leader? How long should a person serve as a team leader? Are team leaders paid? If yes, how?
- How does the principal's role change when teaming is implemented? What new responsibilities does the principal have in a team organization?
- What takes place during team meetings? Should teams meet every day? How much time should be spent discussing students? instruction? curriculum?
- How are teachers assigned to teams? What are some ways this can be done?
- How are encore teachers placed on teams? What are some models indicating how this is done? Why is it important to place all teachers on teams?
- How does a team communicate with other teams? With staff members not on teams? With the administration? With parents?
- What are the costs involved with teaming? Is it more expensive? To what extent?

- What kinds of decisions do teams make that teachers have not made in the past? What problems are encountered in team decision-making?
- How does teaming affect instruction? evaluation and reporting?
- What kind of staff development is necessary to make teaming effective in a middle school?
- What is the research on teaming? Do students learn better? Are teachers happy with teaming? Have schools abandoned teaming?
- What professional resources should be available for teams?
- Where can we go to see quality teams in action?

These questions face middle school staff members in their attempt to understand the concept of teaming. Because change is frightening, it is important to establish the idea that teachers on teams will have a great amount of autonomy in making decisions that affect them and their students. Focusing on the very real " positive possibilities" of teaming can relieve some stress that staff members have about considering this basic change in organizational structure. On the other hand, the efforts required to implement teaming should not be downplayed.

Initial staff development can be accomplished by bringing knowledgeable resource persons to the school, including bringing in a team of teachers from a school with effective teaming, viewing videotapes, attending middle level conferences and reading the many professional resources now available on teaming. Study groups should be formed so that discussions can continue after the inservice meeting. They become a means of sharing readings and results of visits, and holding informal conversations in which apprehensions can be aired.

STEP TWO: VISITING MIDDLE SCHOOLS WITH TEAMING

Early staff development should include visits by staff members and administrators to middle schools with effective teaming programs. Learning from fellow teachers is a powerful way to gain an understanding of teaming. It is best for a group of three or four persons including an administrator to visit any one school. The interchange among those making the visit is valuable, and their impact on the remainder of the faculty is much greater than if only one or two visited a school.

Asking the right questions will provide the right kind of information for sharing among staff members. Below are questions to guide visits to middle schools:

- How many students are in the school?
- How long has this school had teaming?
- How are the teams designed?
- Are teams designed the same way for each grade level?
- Are all teachers on teams? If so, how is this done?
- How many students are on each team?
- How are students assigned to teams?
- How are special education students and their teachers aligned with teams?
- How are team leaders selected?
- Are team leaders remunerated for responsibilities? If so, how?
- What staff development activities were provided when teaming was implemented?
- What happens when team members do not get along?
- What were teacher reactions to teaming when it was first implemented?
- What problems were encountered when teaming was implemented?
- How do you feel about teaming now? What do you like about it? What do you dislike about it?
- How has student learning benefited from teaming?
- What reactions have parents had to teaming?
- What suggestions do you have for us as we consider teaming?

All teachers and administrators should visit at least one middle school and share and discuss the visits in some formal way. If the discussion generates additional questions, or if the answers are not satisfactory, then additional study and discussion will be necessary before implementing teaming.

STEP THREE: TEAM LEADERSHIP

Strong team leadership creates high performance teams. Ideally, team leaders receive special staff development training before teaming is implemented. Their skills will be a significant boost as team members continue with steps four and five described below. Chapter 4 elaborates on team leader staff development.

STEP FOUR: TEAM BUILDING

Helping teachers become fully functioning team members is the next staff development activity. Team building activities should be designed to answer the following questions:
- What is the difference between a group and a team?
- What are the characteristics of an effective team?
- What goals are appropriate for teams?
- What roles should be a part of each team?
- How do team members communicate with one another on the team?
- How do team members communicate with members of other teams?
- What ground rules should be established by each team?
- How will the team make decisions and solve problems?
- What stages of development do teams go through?

These items are discussed in Chapters 6 and 9 as well as in this chapter.

STEP FIVE: ESTABLISHING CONSISTENT EXPECTATIONS FOR STUDENTS ON TEAMS

This staff development activity closely follows team building. It requires teams to initiate discussions about consistent management, instructional, and

learning skill expectations for students. It also provides an opportunity for team members to practice the team-building skills which were introduced in Step Four.

Premises for Setting Expectations

To begin this staff development activity, teams must establish three premises:
- Make each decision on the basis of "What's best for kids." While decisions affect teachers, administrators, and the curriculum, the education of students has to have the highest priority.
- There is more than one good way to do things. Teachers, especially those with experience, must realize there are a variety of effective ways of handling items such as tardiness, late homework, and cheating. While they may be comfortable with strategies they have been using, others can and do work effectively.
- All teachers can change and be effective. Teachers have some uneasiness; however, when they realize that when they are in concert with teammates, a new satisfaction will arise and their sense of professional accomplishment will grow.

When faculty members accept these premises, they are ready to establish tentative expectations for their students. These expectations may change as they implement them and receive feedback from students.

Team Expectations for Students

There are three sets of expectations that must be discussed by team members. They are:
- Classroom management procedures
  These include but are not limited to the following items: tardiness, leaving the classroom, cheating, improper language, put-downs, food and drink in the classroom, required supplies, use of an organizational notebook, book covers, writing of notes, fighting, and name calling.
- Classroom instructional procedures
  These include but are not limited to the following items: grading procedures, late work, makeup work, extra credit, proficiency reports, deficiency reports, homework, and paper headings.

- Learning skills

  These include but are not limited to the following items: reading, writing, speaking, listening, note taking, study skills, information retrieval, test taking, critical thinking, and organization.

Worksheets for these sets of expectations are included in Chapter 10.

Establishing Management and Instructional Expectations

A tested procedure that will work to establish management and instructional expectations is described below.

- Select an item for discussion. Each team member explains the procedure he/she currently uses.
- After sharing these, team members must decide if students will benefit from establishing one procedure that all will follow. If they agree, as they should, that one procedure is better for students than several different procedures, they must decide which procedure will be used. This may mean all will follow one teacher's approach or a new one that is acceptable to all is devised.
- If team members cannot reach agreement in a reasonable amount of time, the item should be put on hold and a new item considered. After all items in these first two categories have been discussed, the team should return to those items where no agreement was reached. When a team has reached agreement on some items, it is usually easier to reach agreement on the more difficult issues. If a team cannot agree to adopt a common procedure or cannot agree on a common procedure, each member will have to continue using the present procedure until the team revisits the issue at a later date.

Establishing Consistent Learning Skills

The enduring importance of possessing learning skills, to be able to be life-long learners, makes this category of great importance. A procedure to follow that will establish consistency in teaching these critical learning skills follows:

- Complete an inventory of learning skills currently taught by each team member. The inventory will determine those skills emphasized in each discipline and the extent to which they are emphasized. Furthermore, developing the inventory will likely reveal skills not taught. Chapter

10 includes an inventory form.
- After completing the inventory, each learning skill is discussed to seek consensus on such questions as the following:
  a. To what extent should this skill to be taught at this grade level?
  b. Should one member or all members teach each of the skills?
  c. How will this skill be taught?
  d. When should this skill be taught? How reinforced?

If the amount of staff development time is limited, teams should concentrate on three items: study skills, note taking, and information retrieval. Normally, these skills are emphasized at the beginning of the school year; therefore, team decisions on these skills should be made prior to the beginning of the school year. The remaining skills can be discussed during common planning time.

Team discussions on classroom management, instructional management, and learning skills usually take between 8-12 hours to complete. Providing released time for teams of teachers is the best means to accomplish this very important task. Summer work on these items is appropriate only if all team members are present.

TEAM MEETING ACTIVITIES

Participating in a common planning period is a new experience for most teachers. Therefore, it is important to consider those activities that will become a part of the daily planning period. Team meeting time is built around the following activities:

Student Concerns

During the first year, student learning, social development, and behavior concerns usually dominate the planning period. Teams should limit their discussion of students to no more than 50 percent of their meeting time. There is a strong tendency to focus primarily on students who are experiencing difficulties; these discussions, however, must include consideration of all students.

Resource Persons

The planning period provides an excellent opportunity to communicate with resource persons. In some middle schools, teachers of students with special needs are full-time team members. When this is not possible, these teachers should attend team meetings on a scheduled basis. The counselor should be scheduled weekly but attends only if his/her services are needed. Media personnel meet with the team monthly to discuss new materials available for instructional purposes or when a new unit is being planned. The school nurse and school psychologist are also involved as needed. The lines of communication are important if the services of resource persons are to be used during the school year.

Some teams use common planning time for parent conferencing. While highly desirable, conferencing with parents must be restricted somewhat so teams can attend to other issues.

Resource persons are valuable for teams. However, team meeting time as well as the time of the resource persons is valuable and limited. Therefore, resource persons should only attend team meetings on invitation.

Student Activities

Providing recognition, social, and recreational activities is an excellent way to create a sense of unity and belonging for students on the team. Teams can use planning time to organize activities to develop an esprit de corps.

Professional Activities

Teams should use at least one planning period every two weeks to discuss professional issues. A person who attended a conference could share information gleaned from the meeting. Teacher might each read a particular article at home and share their reactions during this occasional professional activity period. A team could also decide to read a professional book, discussing a chapter or two every two weeks.

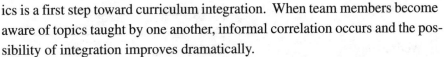

Curriculum

During common planning time, team members share topics they intend to teach and what will be required of students. Sharing requirements will alleviate unintentionally overloading students with tests, projects, or homework. Sharing topics is a first step toward curriculum integration. When team members become aware of topics taught by one another, informal correlation occurs and the possibility of integration improves dramatically.

Teams that have effective leadership are efficient with routine team duties and control the amount of time spent discussing student concerns so they are able to utilize planning time for curriculum improvement. Teams should not be distressed, however, if little planning time is spent on curriculum integration during the first semester or year of teaming. The first year they must concentrate primarily on moving from being just a group to becoming a real team where building collegiality and concern for students' academic and personal welfare is present.

SCHEDULING TEAM MEETING TIME

A weekly or biweekly schedule of activities is imperative if teams aspire to high performance. Knowing what is to occur each day reduces confusion and frustration.

An example of a two-week schedule, presented in Figure 30, can be used as a basis for developing a team's own schedule of activities during the important common planning period.

Figure 30

Schedule of Planning Time Activities

WEEK ONE	WEEK TWO
Monday Special education Review of week	Monday Special education Review of week
Tuesday Counselor visit Discussion of students	Tuesday Counselor visit Discussion of students
Wednesday Social activies Recognition/awards	Wednesday Professional day
Thursday Upcoming content Upcoming requirements	Thursday Upcoming content Upcoming requirements
Friday Discussion of students Parent contact	Friday Discussion of students Parent contact

SUMMARY

There is no substitute for quality staff development when making the change to an interdisciplinary organizational structure within a middle school. Teaming has untold potential for improving teaching and learning and the attitudes of both teachers and students. Staff development efforts must help teachers understand the concept of teaming and its possibilities and help them learn how to become effective team members. Specific activities should be directed toward making evident the opportunities for enhancing learning within this type of organizational structure. It is imperative that the school district provide the support needed for staff development activities. To ensure a quality teaming program, more than a decision to try it and a one-day inservice program is needed. The time and money invested in staff development will pay off in faculty morale and student achievement. ❏

8

Recognizing and Managing Dysfunctional Team Behavior

Most potential teams can become real teams, but not without taking risks involving conflict, trust, interdependence, and hard work.

— Jon Katzenbach and Douglas Smith

T eams will, from time to time, exhibit dysfunctional behaviors and individual team members often will act in nonproductive ways. A healthy team recognizes inappropriate behaviors and takes steps to correct them. While individual members of the team need to be on the watch for symptoms of team problems, it is especially important for the team leader and the principal to be aware of these signs.

SYMPTOMS OF DYSFUNCTIONAL TEAMS

Dysfunctional behaviors generally cluster in four areas: team focus, team leadership, team communication, and team ground rules.

Focus

Chapter 6 identifies the two most important characteristics of effective teams: they have established clear goals and they evidence a commitment to work toward achieving these goals. Deviation from either of these characteristics has severe consequences on team effectiveness. Symptoms indicating a lack of team focus include:

- no established goals or unclear and unrealistic goals
- no specific agenda for team meetings
- no commitment to the concept of teaming or a tapering off of the commitment

- reduction in the quality of the work of the team
- lack of consistency in production with shortcuts sometimes taken
- reports and assignments often late
- inadequate preparation for meetings
- inability to reach closure on any activity
- lack of creativity in team planning

Leadership

As detailed in Chapter 4, the team leader's role has not been clearly defined in many middle schools. Nonproductive team leader behaviors inevitably cause team dysfunction. Furthermore, as indicated in Chapter 5, a middle school principal who does not understand her/his role relative to interdisciplinary teams may also contribute to ineffective team behaviors.

Poor team leadership can cause the following dysfunctional behaviors:
- disorganized meetings that waste time
- wasted meeting time
- no movement toward goals
- inability to make decisions and solve problems
- unwillingness to take risks
- negative feelings toward teaming expressed verbally or non-verbally
- confusion over responsibilities

Communication

To be effective, there must be open communication between team members, with the team leader, between teams, and with the administration. Teams with communication problems show the following symptoms:
- hesitancy when speaking
- hiding true feelings
- blaming others for team problems
- forming cliques and alliances
- hidden agendas
- failing to share information with team members
- a major increase or decrease in verbal communication in meetings
- name calling and stereotyping

Ground Rules

Team operating rules or ground rules govern the behavior of team members. Failure to establish these procedures can result in many difficulties. Teams that have not established ground rules or ignore them exhibit these dysfunctional behaviors:

- no exact starting and ending time
- absenteeism from meetings for trivial reasons
- interruptions of meetings
- no decision-making techniques for resolving difficult issues
- individuals do not adhere to team decisions
- lack of procedures to solve difficult problems
- decisions made with insufficient and/or unreliable information
- decisions made hurriedly and carelessly
- lack of trust
- lack of respect
- defensiveness and rancor when there is disagreement
- lack of patience
- unwillingness to cooperate with one another
- negative and critical behavior
- inadequate support for team members

MANAGING DYSFUNCTIONAL TEAMS

It would be wonderful if, for every dysfunctional behavior of teams or team members, specific procedures were available to remedy the situation. Dealing with these behaviors is similar to working with students who are having difficulties. While a general procedure may work with most students, each student misbehavior must be treated as an individual situation. The same is true with team members and with teams that are not performing up to expectations. The general procedures that follow will suggest to teams, team leaders, and principals ways of helping individuals become effective team members, but the dynamics of the particular situation will require adjustments.

The Team

Effective teams will find gentle ways to remind their members when they have broken ground rules Team-designed sanctions serve as friendly reminders to change one's behavior. Teams have adopted sanctions similar to the following:

- bringing refreshments to the next meeting
- placing a small fine into the team's social fund
- calling time when one individual has been speaking for a long period of time
- accepting any assignment given while absent without a valid reason

These sanctions serve more as reminders than punishment but do help the team from becoming dysfunctional.

Discussing the offending behavior as a team is helpful. For example, if several people are late for team meetings, the team should revisit the ground rule. The team may decide to change the starting time to help all members be on time or help one another find ways to be prompt.

The Team Leader

Dealing with an issue in which several team members have been guilty of transgressions is much easier than when the offense involves one individual. Teams that have a problem-solving technique for handling curricular or instructional issues can use this procedure for transgressions against team rules.

A strong team leader knows how to help a team resolve problems. The leader is aware of a range of options for handling team problems such as the following:

- support the team in invoking a sanction
- review ground rules with the team
- structure the meeting so all members are involved in the discussion.
- structure a project to involve all members
- devise an agenda with limited time allocated to each item
- talk privately to the person whose behavior is a problem

If the team leader is not able to resolve a problem, assistance can be sought from other team leaders. They may have dealt successfully with a comparable problem or have ideas to offer. The team leader can also discuss the issue with the principal. Comments on the principal's role follows.

The Principal

The principal plays an important role in handling ineffective team behaviors. First, the principal must make sure teams understand dysfunctional team behaviors. Small items such as coming late to meetings may be a way of life in a building, and arriving late for a team meeting is not seen as a problem. Helping team members understand and accept the concept of a "team" and those activities that will detract from the team's effective performance falls on the shoulders of the principal. Second, the principal must empower the team to solve its own problems, by encouraging team members to deal directly with the problems and/or working with the team leader to resolve the issues. Third, everyone must understand that properly functioning teams are the expectation, and the principal will take whatever action necessary to ensure they do so.

When the team cannot resolve the problem, the principal must intervene. This can be done in a number of ways:

- meet with the entire team to discuss the situation and make recommendations directly to the team
- deal separately with the person causing the problem. If the problem is severe, use such school district procedures as official reprimands

- reorganize the team by changing team members
- assist the dysfunctional team member in finding a non-team position in another school within the district
- assist the dysfunctional team member to find a position in another school district

While some of these actions are severe, the principal cannot tolerate dysfunctional teams or ineffective team members, for they impact directly on the welfare and achievement of students.

CONFLICT RESOLUTION

Conflict within teams is inevitable if the team is a growing, thriving unit. Conflict can be positive, allowing team members to explore new ideas and test opinions. Effective teams are not afraid of conflicting opinions realizing the benefits that can arise from them. However, unnecessary and excessive conflict can drain the energies of team members. If conflict brings such tension to the team that performance is affected, it must be resolved.

Signs of Conflict

It is important that the team leader and team members recognize signs of conflict. Some are clear and easily recognizable such as those listed below:

- Personal attacks on other team members
- Not listening carefully, jumping to conclusions
- Continuous postponement of decisions
- Not willing to move from a position on a topic.

Some signs of conflict occur early and are more subtle. Examples of these less obvious signs follow.

- Increased or decreased talk on particular topics
- Absences or tardiness from team meetings
- Satirical statements presumably made in jest about one another
- Difficulty with decision making.

Handling Team Conflict

Five strategies that teams may use when dealing with conflict are described below. Each of them is valuable in particular circumstances.

- Ignore or deny that a conflict exists
  This occurs when the team leader or team members feel uncomfortable dealing directly with conflict. If the conflict remains at a low level, the team may be able to operate without addressing the issue. Unfortunately, conflict may deepen and become more difficult to resolve at a later date.

- Agree to disagree
  This strategy, known as *smoothing*, is a means of retaining the personal relationships that exist on the team but avoiding issues that cause friction between team members. If the issues do not have negative effects on teaching and learning on the team, smoothing is a reasonable strategy. However, if conflict arises over a major issue such as teaching integrated units, then smoothing is inappropriate.

- Compromise
  Compromise results when both parties move from their position in order to gain group consensus. In the decision-making process, compromise is labeled *lose-lose* because each party must give up something to gain a solution. Neither party is completely satisfied with the decision, but the problem is resolved and the team can move ahead. The attitudes displayed by those at odds is the key to progress.

- Forcing
  This procedure, done through voting, drives people to accept another's view to resolve a conflict. Voting results in a *win-lose* situation and may deepen the gulf between members.

- Problem solving
  Problem solving requires people to cooperate in serious discussions in order to reach a mutually agreeable solution. Steps for solving problems to reach *win-win* situations are presented in Chapter 9.

Team Leader Role in Managing Conflict

The team leader plays a central role in helping resolve conflicts. The leader is in a difficult position because he/she is a member of the instructional team and a colleague of the team members. Furthermore, few team leaders have been trained in conflict resolution procedures and may feel very uncomfortable attempting to adjudicate team conflicts. Team leaders must assess their level of comfort with conflict resolution and seek outside assistance when appropriate. Talking over a situation with the principal may provide suggestions for the direction to be taken by the team leader. If the problem is severe, the principal may decide to handle the situation without the team leader or seek outside assistance.

When the team leader sees signs of conflict, the following questions should be considered before attempting to resolve the conflict:

- Is the problem of such a nature that resolution is necessary?
- Could the team agree to disagree without causing harm to the team's ability to meet its goals?
- Can a compromise be reached on the conflict?
- What is likely to result if a vote is taken on the issue?
- Should the conflict be resolved by using a problem-solving procedure?

These questions parallel the five strategies for handling team conflict: ignoring, agreeing to disagree, compromising, forcing, and problem solving. Responding to the questions will provide the starting point for dealing with the conflict. Team leaders should seek assistance if uncertain of the direction to take in helping the team resolve the conflict.

SUMMARY

Teams must be aware of the fact that some conflict is normal and even positive, but it can grow to be disabling. The team leader and principal must continuously monitor the progress of the team and the behavior of individual members to ensure early detection of problems. Knowing when to intercede and how to help members resolve their differences is an important role of the team leader. A team that can resolve conflicts will be a highly productive team. ❏

9

Decision Making and Problem Solving

Obvious advantages of a group decision-making and problem-solving process are that it expands the range of available options, enhances the quality of the solutions, and increases commitment among those involved.

— Glenn H. Varney

D ecision making and problem solving are crucial skills a team needs to become a high performance team. These two skills take on new meaning when applied to a team rather than an individual. In this chapter, decision making and problem solving will be explored and several tools presented that assist in problem solving.

DECISION MAKING

Most team decisions can be made informally. However, when difficult issues arise, it is important that the team has an agreed upon decision-making procedure in place.

Making decisions is much easier when working independently than when one works with others. Decisions made by a team have to reflect the concerns, biases, and experiences of each member. Bridging the beliefs of each individual in order to satisfy all involved in the decision-making process is often a difficult task.

Decision making, whether by an individual or by a team, follows a process. The initial task is to identify as many ideas and options as possible, then to reduce the number of them, and, finally, to reach agreement on one or more solutions. The steps in the decision-making process are described below.

Generating Ideas

The first step in the decision-making process is to generate as many ideas, options, and suggested solutions as possible. If only two ideas are put forth and neither is a good idea, then it is inevitable that the final decision will be less than adequate. Therefore, the task of the team is to brainstorm the largest possible number of ideas.

Brainstorming is governed by several rules:

- No value judgments are made on any ideas presented because they might inhibit people from creative thinking.
- The wilder the ideas, the better, for while a particular idea may never be implemented, it may spawn another imaginative idea.
- The number of ideas initially is more important than the quality of the ideas.

Brainstorming can be done in a variety of ways. Three approaches are described on the next page.

- Each person takes several minutes to prepare his/her own list of ideas, then presents them to the entire group.
- Each person, in turn, initiates an idea which is added to the list.
- Any member of the team is free to call out ideas in a random fashion.

Reducing the Number of Ideas

The second step is to reduce the many suggestions to a manageable number in one of several ways. Just prior to beginning this task, however, the list of brainstormed ideas should be cleaned up by eliminating duplicates and clarifying vague items. Several well-known techniques are described below.

- Multi-voting

  In multi-voting, members of the team select their top choices from the total list. The number of choices is somewhat arbitrary but may depend on the length of the list. This will produce a set of items receiving significant number of votes and identifies items receiving limited or no votes. After some discussion, a second round of voting further reduces the number of ideas. Voting and discussion can continue until the same items receive the same number of votes.

Example of Multi-voting
An eighth grade team is attempting to identify
a service project for their team

Step 1:　The team brainstorms 30 service projects; they decide to reduce this list to five or fewer items.

Step 2:　They agree that, in the first round of voting, members will select their top ten projects and that items receiving few or no votes will be deleted from the list.

Step 3:　The voting is done and the results tallied and discussed.

Step 4:　Steps two and three are repeated until the same items receive the same number of votes.

- Nominal group technique

  This technique requires team members to select their top choices from the list but also to prioritize the items selected. If each member selects four items from the brainstormed list, then each of the four items is rated one to four with four indicating the highest priority. This will produce a reduced list and identify the priority of each of the items selected.

Example of Nominal Group Technique

A seventh-grade team is attempting to identify

a field trip for their team

Step 1:   The team brainstorms sixteen possible field trips. They decide to reduce the number to four.

Step 2:   On a sheet of paper, identify each of the sixteen items by the letter A, B, C, etc.

Step 3:   Each member selects four items from the list of sixteen and places the letter of that item on a slip of paper.

Step 4:   The four items selected are ranked from four to one (highest ranked item receives a four, the next a three, etc.) and the ranking placed on the slip of paper.

Step 5:   Using the master list of items, obtain the ranking from each team member. Place on the master list and add up the ranking points. For example, item A may have received ranking points of 3, 2, and 4 for a total of 9; item B ranking points of 1 and 3 for a total of 4.

Step 6.   Determine which items have the highest rating. Discuss the results and do the procedure again to reduce the number further if necessary.

- Dot technique

  This technique, a variation of the nominal group procedure, entails developing a selected list of items from the master list that indicates the priorities of the choices. *Stick-em* dots of different colors are used, each color representing a different value. Members "spend" their dots on ideas and values are totaled.

Example of the Dot Technique

A sixth-grade team is attempting to identify
a set of goals for their team for the ensuing school year.

Step 1:   The team brainstorms a number of items.

Step 2:   Each member receives three stick-em dots, one blue, one
red, one yellow. A red dot equals three points, blue equals
two, and yellow equals one.

Step 3:   Team members "spend" their three dots by placing them
on the master list of brainstormed goals. If a person feels
strongly about one item, all three dots can be placed on
that item, or the three dots can be spread over three items.

Step 4:   Tally the value of the dots placed on each item.

Step 5:   Discuss the results; repeat the dot procedure to reduce
the number further if needed. All items receiving at least
one red dot (someone's highest ranking) should remain
on the list for further discussion and voting.

Each of the three techniques is a procedure to reduce the number of brainstormed items to a more manageable list. From this new list a final choice or
choices will be made. In all cases, free discussion should accompany the voting lest the procedure become cold and mechanical.

Consensus Decision Making

Attempting to reach a decision that will satisfy all members of a team is termed
consensus decision making. Reaching consensus requires everyone to volun-
tarily accept and support the final decision. While some members may not be
completely satisfied with the decision, they will agree to support it.

Fortunately, most decisions by middle school teams can be reached satisfac-
torily without going through the full consensus procedure. Consensus decision
making can be a long but thoughtful process. Time spent in making the decision is offset, however, by greater satisfaction and agreement in the implementation of the decision.

The following principles must be followed to reach consensus:

• Each person must fully understand the items being discussed.

- Each person must be frank about his/her views. There can be no hidden agendas. Views, even if unpopular, must be heard thoughtfully, thoroughly, and without prejudice.
- Each person must listen actively, discuss openly, and be creative in his/her thinking.
- Each person must think and act beyond self interests placing the welfare of the team first.

The following steps are a guide to reaching consensus on a decision:

- Step One: Brainstorm a list of ideas and then reduce that number using one of the procedures described above.
- Step Two: For each of the 3-5 items remaining on the list, complete an analysis listing the strengths and weaknesses or advantages and disadvantages of each item.

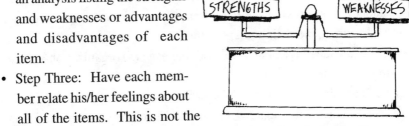

- Step Three: Have each member relate his/her feelings about all of the items. This is not the time to withhold feelings only to have them surface in the faculty room. The team leader must make sure that all members makes their feelings known on each item.
- Step Four: If at this point a particular idea has not surfaced as agreeable to all, determine if more than one item under consideration is appropriate.
- Step Five: Try to reach a decision. Identify those ideas on the list that all can agree should be eliminated. Continue discussing the items that remain. If one person is vehemently opposed to an idea acceptable to remaining members, seek to have that person "stand aside" for a period of time while the more popular view is implemented or piloted. Here is where authorities on consensus decision making differ. Some suggest that if one or more items are not agreeable to all team members, the process should begin anew to try to determine a mutually agreeable decision. Others suggest that "practical consensus" should be called into play and a vote taken to determine the course of action.

Teachers can come to agreement on most simple items without using any formal decision-making procedure. However, team members should be skilled in decision making for those few difficult decisions. Becoming good decision makers takes study and practice. If interdisciplinary teams in middle level schools are to move to a higher level of efficiency and effectiveness, the skill of consensus decision making should be learned and used.

PROBLEM SOLVING

Middle school teams encounter problems that need resolution in such areas as the following: (1) students – resolving the issue of frequent absences or continually missing assignments; (2) communication – connecting with some parents about the progress of their children; (3) curriculum – agreeing on the extent and form of thematic units; (4) instruction – meeting the needs of a students with a wide range of abilities and interests; (5) organization – eliminating tacking on teams.

Teams in their initial stages of formation may struggle with a process to resolve such issues while mature teams have developed a problem-solving process that can be applied to any situation facing the team. Teams that are comfortable with a process will not fear problems but will systematically apply the process and continue their work without allowing a problem to create dissension within the team.

The problem-solving process is quite generic. Most writers on the topic agree that the process involves five steps:

Step One: Define the Problem
The first and most important step is to define the problem clearly. On the surface this may appear to be a relatively simple step. Yet, unless the problem is succinctly defined, a team may end up with a great solution to a different problem. It is, therefore, essential for the team to respond to such questions as the following:

- How does each of us define the problem?
- How often is the problem occurring and under what circumstances?
- What information do we have about the causes of the problem?
- Who is affected and to what extent?

A key to defining the problem is to look beyond the symptoms to uncover the "real" problem. For example, a team concerned about the number of missing assignments, upon investigating the situation, discovers that the student's assignments are missing only the Fridays and Mondays when the youngster spends a weekend with his/her non-custodial parent. Thus, the real problem to be resolved is how to ensure that homework is completed on days surrounding those weekends or how to make adjustments in the requirements.

It is helpful if team members are aware of tools available to help define the true causes of a problem. Being comfortable with tools such as the *cause and effect diagram (fish bone), force field analysis*, and *pareto charts* is advantageous for the team. These tools are described later in this chapter.

Once the problem has been clearly defined, the team is ready to move on to the next step.

Step Two: Identify Solutions

The more potential solutions identified to resolve a problem, the better the chances that the solution selected will be an effective one. To ensure a lengthy list of potential solutions to the problem, the team might invite others such as the school nurse, guidance counselor, and attendance officer to be involved in this process. The knowledge and unique experiences of these people, can assist the team in finding creative solutions. Continuing the example of the student who is missing assignments after spending a weekend with a non-custodial parent, the counselor, social worker, and perhaps both parents would be able to generate worthwhile solutions. Often the student will have valuable ideas that should be considered. Brainstorming within the team and/or with selected members is an excellent way to generate a list of possible solutions.

Step Three: Evaluate and Select the Best Solution

Prior to choosing the best solution, it is imperative that the criteria for the solution be defined. Questions that guide this discussion are:

- Will it have a long-term effect on the problem, or is it just a short-term solution?
- Can the solution be managed by the team, or is it beyond the expertise of the team?
- What time limits are imposed on the solution?
- What resources are needed to implement the solution, and will these resources be available?
- Will the solution be an acceptable one for members of the team and any other people who are involved?
- What are the risks involved in a particular solution?
- Does a particular solution create additional problems?

When the criteria have been established, the team begins the decision-making process including brainstorming, reducing the number of solutions, and selecting the best one.

Step Four: Implement the Selected Decision

It will be advantageous if all members have agreed upon the solution, because all must be involved in implementing the decision. Making sure that all members understand their roles in carrying out the solution will reduce the possibility for confusion. The timeline for implementation must be developed to ensure a logical and effective movement toward a resolution. Finally, the procedures for evaluating the progress of the resolution must be selected so that important data can be collected.

Step Five: Evaluate the Solution and Adjust

This step includes collecting data on the progress of the resolution, evaluating the data, and making necessary adjustments in the process. Teams may consider using one or more of the following problem-solving tools to collect and analyze the data.

PROBLEM-SOLVING TOOLS

The steps of defining the problem and evaluating the solution include collecting and analyzing data. These two items are often treated lightly or disregarded when attempting to resolve problems, yet they yield important information that can have a very positive effect on identifying and implementing solutions.

A variety of procedures can be used to collect and analyze data. Some emphasize the collection of data, others the analysis of data, and many foster both collection and analysis. For each procedure, several examples of its use with teaming are presented.

Affinity Diagram	An affinity diagram is a technique to help generate a number of ideas and place them in similar groupings. It might be used when brainstorming service projects or social activities for students.
Brainstorming	Brainstorming generates ideas from members of a group. Teams may wish to brainstorm ideas for thematic units, ways to handle particular discipline problems, or places to take students on a field trip.
Checklist	A checklist allows an observer to record the presence or absence of an item or process. Teams may use these to record assignments completed or parent attendance at conferences.
Fishbone Diagram	A fishbone diagram is a graphic display of the causes for a particular problem. It is developed through a brainstorming process. Determining the causes for certain student behaviors or reasons for teacher tardiness to team meetings are two examples where teams might use a fishbone diagram.

Flow Chart

A flow chart provides information on the flow or sequence of a process. Flowcharting would help a team view its process for organizing and completing a field trip or the process used to develop a team budget.

Forced Field

Forced field analysis helps identify the forces that drive two sides of an issue. Viewing both the driving and restraining forces assists with strengthening the driving and reducing the restraining forces. A discussion of tracking and inclusion would be helped with this analysis tool.

Mapping

Familiar to most teachers, this procedure provides a pictorial view of a large number of ideas and the relationship of those ideas to one another. Developing an integrated unit of instruction and a set of activities for instructional contracts for students are two uses of this procedure.

Pareto Chart

A pareto chart is a form of a bar graph which ranks the data showing items that occur most frequently. This type of chart would help a team decide which data have the greatest impact on the issue. It could be used to evaluate reasons for parents' lack of involvement in middle schools or types of misbehavior most prevalent during periods of the day.

Questionnaires

Questionnaires or other survey instruments are used to collect data from a large group of people. Teams may use these to secure student perceptions of projects, field trips, and

Run Chart

team procedures. Parents can share their perceptions of a variety of team activities through a questionnaire.

Determining trends over a period of time can be facilitated by the development of a run chart. Data are graphed within a time period to determine changes in a process. A team could develop a run chart to observe a student's absences over a period of time or the changes in behavior of a student before and after a change in policy.

Scatter Diagram

Scatter diagrams are excellent for studying the relationships between two variables. Studying the relationship between reading and mathematics scores or a new style of instruction and student performance would suggest the use of a scatter diagram to interpret the data.

Three of these procedures are used extensively in the business world but seldom seen in the field of education. They are described in more detail below.

Fishbone Diagram

The fishbone diagram is so named because, when developed, it resembles the spine of a fish. The purpose of the diagram is to detail the causes of a problem under consideration. To construct a fishbone diagram, follow the steps below.

1. Gain agreement on the issue under consideration.
2. Identify the major categories of concerns. Examples are people, methods, materials, resources, building, and environment. Create as many as needed. Connect these ribs to the backbone of the fishbone chart.
3. For each category, brainstorm causes of the issue under discussion and place those items on the appropriate ribs. Sometimes it is effective to

brainstorm the entire list of causes before placing them on the chart. Also, some causes may fit on more than one rib.

4. Analyze the information on the fishbone to determine those causes that appear in several locations. If it is necessary to select one cause, use the procedures outlined in the decision-making section of this chapter.

An example of a fishbone diagram is provided in Figure 31. The issue in this example is to determine the causes of misbehavior when students are sent to the library. After completing the diagram, it would appear that the major cause for student misbehavior centers around the problems with resources available to students. The fishbone diagram helps to identify the causes of this problem.

Figure 31

Fishbone Diagram

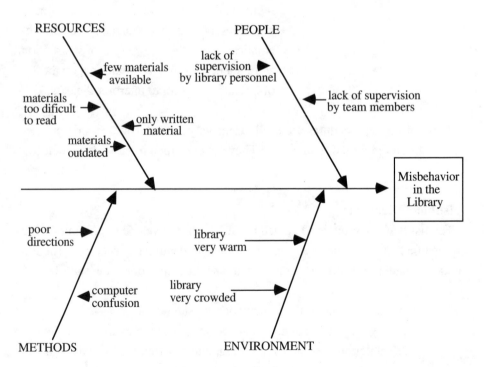

Forced Field

This procedure helps visualize the positives and negatives of an issue. To complete the forced field analysis, follow the steps below:

1. Draw a "T" on a large piece of newsprint. Above the horizontal line, write the goal or desired change.
2. Above the horizontal line and above the left portion of the "T", write "Driving Forces" and on the right "Restraining Forces."
3. Begin a brainstorming session listing all possible driving and restraining forces.
4. When all items have been listed, focus the discussion on eliminating the restraining forces. Rather than strengthening the driving forces, movement toward the goal can be facilitated by reducing, eliminating, or accommodating the restraining forces.

An example of a forced field analysis is shown in Figure 32. The issue under consideration is the elimination of tracking in the middle school.

Figure 32

Forced Field Analysis

Driving Forces	Restraining Forces
Research doesn't support tracking	Meets the needs of gifted students
Unequal treatment of students	Meets the needs of students who
Results in dumbed down	learn slowly
curriculum for slower sections	The way it has always been done
No leaders in some classes	High school demands it
Harder to teach	Easier to teach
Many parents don't like it	
Some parents like it	
Makes scheduling very difficult	

Pareto Chart

A Pareto chart displays data in graphic form showing the frequency of each set of data. It indicates the relative importance of each category and helps the viewer focus on those items having the greatest influence on the data – the vital few. To create a Pareto chart

1. construct a bar graph with categories on the horizontal axis and frequency on the vertical axis, and then

2. place the category with the greatest frequency on the left and continue to the category with the smallest frequency on the right.

When graphed, it is easy to determine the category that contributes most to the problem or solution. Variations include graphing the data before and after a change in a process or break any category into sub-units forming linked Pareto charts.

An example is shown in Figure 33. Data collected represent referrals to the office during the eight periods of the day. From the Pareto chart, it is easy to see that most referrals come from period four, just before lunch, next highest is the last period of the day with the least number of referrals coming in period one.

Figure 33

Pareto Chart

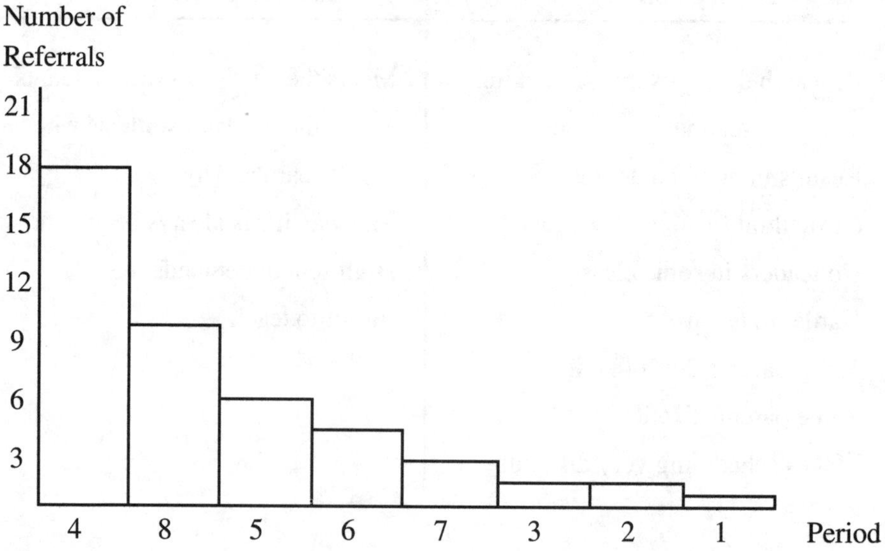

Number of Referrals

Summary

Effective teams develop procedures that assist them when there is a need to resolve difficult problems. Too often, problems are hurriedly decided resulting in no gains, short-term gains, or exacerbation of the problem. Developing a decision-making and problem-solving process that all team members understand and support goes a long way in helping team members achieve a sense of satisfaction in their ability to resolve difficult issues. Problem solving tools will help teams make wise decisions based on data. Defining the problem, identifying solutions, evaluating and selecting the best solution, implementing the decision, evaluating the solutions, and adjusting are the steps that all teams must master to be effective. ❏

10

Resources

BOOKS

Auvine, B., Densmore, B., Extrom, M., Poole, S., & Shanklin, M. (1977). *Manual for group facilitators.* Madison, WI: The Center for Conflict Resolution.

Bader, G. E., Bloom, A. E., & Chang, R. Y. (1994). *Measuring team performance.* Irvine, CA: Richard Chang Associates.

Bennis, W., & Goldsmith, J. (1994). *Learning to lead.* Reading, MA: Addison-Wesley.

Chang, R. Y. (1994). *Building a dynamic team.* Irvine, CA: Richard Chang Associates.

Chang, R. Y. (1994). *Success through teamwork.* Irvine, CA: Richard Chang Associates.

Clark, S. N., & Clark, D. C. (1994). *Restructuring the middle level school.* Albany: State University of New York Press.

Fields, J. C. (1993). *Total quality for schools: A suggestion for American education.* Milwaukee, WI: ASQC Quality Press.

Fisher, K. (1993). *Leading self-directed work teams.* New York: McGraw-Hill Inc.

Harrington-Mackin, D. (1994). *The team building tool kit: Tips, tactics, and rules for effective work place teams.* New York: American Management Association.

Ishikawa, K. (1994). *Guide to quality control.* White Plains, NY: Quality Resources.

Kayser, T. A. (1994). *Team power.* New York: Irwin.

Katzenback, J. R., & Smith, D. K. (1993). *The wisdom of teaming.* Boston: Harvard Business School Press.

Kelly, P. K. (1994). *Team decision-making techniques*. Irvine, CA: Richard Chang Associates, Inc.

Klubnik, J. P., & Greenwood, P. F. (1994). *The team-based problem solver.* New York: Irwin.

Lounsbury, J. H. (Ed.) (1992). *Connecting the curriculum through interdisciplinary instruction*. Columbus, OH: National Middle School Association.

Maddux, R. B. (1992). *Team building: An exercise in leadership*. Menlo Park, CA: Crisp.

Maginn, M. D. (1994). *Effective teamwork*. New York: Business One Irwin/Mirror Press.

Parker, G. M. (1990). *Team players and teamwork*. San Francisco: Jossey-Bass.

Quick, T. L. (1992). *Successful team building*. New York: American Management Association.

Rees, F. (1991). *How to lead work teams*. San Diego, CA: Pfeiffer and Company.

Rottier, J., Landon, G., & Rush, L. (1995). *The middle level schools in Wisconsin: Growth from 1989 to 1994*. Madison, WI: Wisconsin Department of Public Instruction.

Saint, S., & Lawson, J. R. (1994). *Rules for reaching consensus*. San Diego, CA: Pfeiffer & Company.

Scholtes, P. R. (1992). *The team handbook: How to use teams to improve quality*. Madison, WI: Joiner Associates.

Schurr, S. L. (1992). *How to evaluate your middle school*. Columbus, OH: National Middle School Association.

The memory jogger for education. (1994). Methuen, MA: GOAL/QPC.

Valentine, J.,Clark, D., Irvine, J. L., Keefe, J. W., & Melton, G. (1993). *Leadership in middle level education, Volume I: A national survey of middle level leaders and schools*. Reston, VA: National Association of Secondary School Principals.

Whitmore, J. (1994). *Coaching for performance: A practical guide to growing your own skills*. San Diego, CA: Pfeiffer & Company.

Williams, R. B. (1993). *More than 50 ways to build team consensus*. Palatine, IL: IRI/Skylight.

Zander, A. (1994). *Making groups effective*. San Francisco: Jossey-Bass.

ARTICLES

George, P. S. (1982). Interdisciplinary team organization: four operational phases. *Middle School Journal, 13*(3), 10-13.

Kain, D. L. (1993). Helping teams succeed: an essay review of groups that work (and those that don't): creating conditions for effective team-work. *Middle School Journal, 24*(4), 25-31.

Pickler, G. (1987). The evolutionary development of interdisciplinary teams. *Middle School Journal,18*(2), 6-7.

Rottier, J. (1996). The principal and teaming: unleashing the power of collaboration. *Schools in the Middle, 5*(4), 31-36

Smith, H. W. (1991). Guide teaming development. *Middle School Journal. 22*(5), 21-23.

OTHER SOURCES

Lyons Middle School. *Interdisciplinary teaming–rookies in a superbowl year.* (1990). Paper presented at National Middle School Conference, San Diego, CA.

EVALUATION INSTRUMENTS

The following sources provide team assessment instruments.

Bader, G. E., Bloom, A. E., & Chang, R. Y. (1994). *Measuring team performance.* Irvine, CA: Richard Chang Associates.

This book focuses on the concept of team evaluation with chapters on quantitative and qualitative measures and information on interpreting the results. It contains the following reproducible assessment forms: "Team Measurement Decision Checklist," "Team Success Survey" using a seven-point continuum, "Meeting Effectiveness Survey" using a three-point continuum, and "Peer Feedback Survey" with a five-point continuum. No data provided on instrument development.

Chang, R. Y. (1994). *Building a dynamic team.* Irvine, CA: Richard Chang Associates.

This book contains a twelve-item instrument referred to as "Character-istics of a Dynamic Team." It has seven numeric responses with "7" indicating the team is exceptional and "1" meaning it is deficient. No data provided on instrument development.

Klubnik, J. P., & Greenwood, P. F. (1994). *The team-based problem solver.* New York: Irwin.

This book has a twelve-question team process checklist. Responses include "yes," " no," and "somewhat" and a place for comments. In addition, there are four sets of eight to fifteen questions focusing on the team process during the problem solving cycle. The four categories are "ongoing meeting checks," "helping a team through a blockage," "items to use at the end of the process," "and questions to check on individual differences." No data provided on instrument development.

Quick, T. L. (1992). *Successful team building.* New York: American Management Association.

This author presents a peer evaluation form to help the team leader evaluate each member. There are ten items with a ten-point continuum measuring the progress of the group toward its stated goals. No data provided on instrument development.

Rottier, J. (1992). *Interdisciplinary organization.* Eau Claire, WI: Center for Middle Level Assessment.

The instrument on interdisciplinary organization contains 87 items focusing on seven aspects of teaming: team planning, communication, curriculum and instruction, interpersonal relations, team functions, effects on students, and public relations. Four levels of agreement are available for each response. A version exists for the professional staff, parents, and students. Instruments were validated nationally, tested in middle schools, and are available for purchase. Includes scoring services.

Schurr, S. L. (1992). *How to evaluate your middle school.* Columbus, OH: National Middle School Association.

Designed for a faculty to do a relatively informal evaluation. Three forms relative to teaming are presented. The first is a "team self-checklist" with thirty items. Responses are "always," "frequently," "infrequently," and "never" with room for comments. The second is a "team meeting observation form" with responses of "yes" and "no" and room for comments. The final is a "team member interview form" with twelve open-ended questions. No data provided on instrument development.

FORMS

The Classroom Management Procedures Form is a guide for teams as they determine team procedures for classroom management concerns.

Classroom Management Procedures *"What's Best for Kids"*	
Item	Team Procedures
1. Tardiness	

2. Leaving the Classroom
 	
    A. Lockers
 	
    B. Bathroom
 	
    C. IMC
 	
    D. Office
 	
    E. Nurse
 	
    F. Guidance office
 	
    G. Water fountain	

3. Cheating
 	
    A. Tests
 	
    B. Daily work	

Item	Team Procedures
4. Positive Reinforcement A. Student recognition B. Birthdays C. Calls to parents D. Team activities	
5. Punishments A. Detention B. Loss of privileges C. Extra work D. Lowering academic marks	
6. Other A. Poor language B. Food in classroom C. Chewing gum D. Books not covered E. Notewriting F. Organizational notebook G. Required supplies H. Other	

The Classroom Instructional Procedures Form is a guide for teams as they determine team procedures for instructional concerns.

Classroom Instructional Procedures *"What's Best for Kids"*	
Item	Team Procedures

1. Evaluation
 	
    A. Numerical/letter grades
 	
    B. Grading scale
 	
    C. Extra credit
 	
    D. Late work
 	
    E. Make-up work
 	
    F. Proficiency reports
 	
    G. Deficiency reports
 	
    H. Grading adjustments
        (Special needs students)
 	
    I. Other	

2. Homework
 	
    A. Frequency of
        assignments
 	
    B. Length of assignments
 	
    C. Evaluation of homework
 	
        1. Percentage correct
 	
        2. Based on effort
 	
    D. Paper headings	

The Teaming Learning Skills Analysis Chart serves as a guide for teams as they decide common procedures for teaching learning skills.

Team Learning Skills Analysis *"What's Best for Kids"*	
Item	Team Procedures
1. Reading	
2. Writing	
3. Listening	
4. Speaking	
5. Note Taking	
6. Study Skills	
7. Information Retrieval	
8. Thinking/Problem Solving	
9. Test Taking	
10. Organization	

The Analysis of Learning Skills chart provides a structure for teams as they determine which learning skills are taught by each teacher on the team.

Analysis of Learning Skills

Skills	Reading	Writing	Listening	Speaking	Note Taking	Study Skills	Information Retrieval	Problem Solving	Test Taking	Organization
Math										
Science										
Social Studies										
Language Arts										
Reading										
Art										
Music										
Family & Consumer Education										
Technology Education										
Physical Education										
Foreign Language										
Other										

This Two-Week Planning Cycle form is used by teams as they plan activities for their common planning time.

Two-Week Planning Cycle **Team Planning Time** *"What's Best for Kids"*	
Week One	Week Two
Monday	Monday
Tuesday	Tuesday
Wednesday	Wednesday
Thursday	Thursday
Friday	Friday

References

Carnegie Council on Adolescent Development's Task Force on Young Adolescents. (1989). *Turning points: Preparing American youth for the 21st century.* Washington, DC: Carnegie Council on Adolescent Development.

Covey, S. R. (1989). *The 7 habits of highly effective people.* New York: Simon and Schuster.

Craig, J. S. (1995). Quality through site-based scheduling. *Middle School Journal, 27*(2), 17-22.

Fullan, Michael G. (1991). The *Meaning of Educational Change.* New York: Teachers College Press.

George, P., & Shewey, K. (1994). *New evidence for the middle school.* Columbus, OH: National Middle School Association.

Katzenback, J. R., & Smith, D. K. (1993). *The wisdom of teaming.* Boston: Harvard Business School Press.

Kayser, T. A. (1994). *Team power.* New York: Irwin.

Martin, Don. (1993). *TeamThink.* New York: Penguin Books.

Oakley, E., & Krug, D. (1991). *Enlightened leadership–getting to the heart of change.* New York: Simon and Schuster.

Scholtes, P. R. (1992). *The team handbook: how to use teams to improve quality.* Madison, WI: Joiner Associates.

Team leader job description. (1994). Bonduel Middle School, Bonduel, WI.

Tuckman, B. W. (1967). Developmental sequence in small groups *Psychological Bulletin, 63* (6), 384-399.

Varney, Glenn H. (1989). *Building productive teams.* San Francisco: Jossey-Bass Publishers.

NATIONAL MIDDLE SCHOOL ASSOCIATION

National Middle School Association was established in 1973 to serve as a voice for professionals and others interested in the education of young adolescents. The Association has grown rapidly and now enrolls members in all fifty states, the Canadian provinces, and forty-two other nations. In addition, fifty-three state, regional, and provincial middle school associations are official affiliates of NMSA.

NMSA is the only association dedicated exclusively to the education, development, and growth of young adolescents. Membership is open to all. While middle level teachers and administrators make up the bulk of the membership, central office personnel, college and university faculty, state department officials, other professionals, parents, and lay citizens are also actively involved in supporting our single mission – improving the educational experiences of 10-15 year olds. This open membership is a particular strength of NMSA.

The Association provides a variety of services, conferences, and materials in fulfilling its mission. In addition to *Middle School Journal*, the movement's premier professional journal, the Association publishes *Research in Middle Level Education Quarterly*, a wealth of books and monographs, videos, a general newsletter, an urban education newspaper, and occasional papers. The Association's highly acclaimed annual conference, which has drawn over 10,000 registrants in recent years, is held in the fall.

For information about NMSA and its many services contact the Headquarters at 2600 Corporate Exchange Drive, Suite 370, Columbus, Ohio 43231, TELEPHONE 800-528-NMSA, FAX 614-895-4750.